THAMES TIDEWAY
Vol 6 English Estuaries Series

ROBERT SIMPER

Published by Creekside Publishing 1997
ISBN 0 9519927 6 7
Printed by The Lavenham Press Ltd
Lavenham, Suffolk

By the same author

Over Snape Bridge (1967)
Woodbridge & Beyond (1972)
East Coast Sail (1972)
Scottish Sail (1974)
North East Sail (1975)
British Sail (1977)
Victorian & Edwardian Yachting from Old Photographs (1978)
Gaff Sail (1979)
Traditions of East Anglia (1980)
Suffolk Show (1981)
Britain's Maritime Heritage (1982)
Sail on the Orwell (1982)
Beach Boats of Britain (1984)
Sail: The Surviving Tradition (1984)
East Anglian Coast and Waterways (1985)
Suffolk Sandlings (1986)
The Deben River (1992)
The River Orwell and the River Stour (1993)
Rivers Alde, Ore and Blyth (1994)
Woodbridge: Pictorial History (1995)
Essex Rivers and Creeks (1995)
Norfolk Rivers and Harbours (1996)

CONTENTS

Cover: The replica bark *Endeavour* approaching
Tower Bridge (author)

INTRODUCTION

The Thames is a very political river, its past and future arouses great passions, but I hope this work adds a little to the record of a truly great estuary. The purpose of this book is to recall the tidal River Thames of the past, particularly the ways of the working river which have been swept away. It is not possible to record the history of every part of this mighty river in detail. It is more a case of following the trends and using a few photographs to tell a vast story.

Originally the Thames was a wide shallow river with vast areas of ooze and saltings on either shore. From the medieval period onwards the saltings were walled off to create grazing marsh and this confined the channel to its present course. In the nineteenth century the channel was dredged deeper to allow the largest ships in the world to get up to the docks. As the population grew, houses were built on low lying land which were liable to flood in abnormally high tides, particularly in 1928 and 1953 when flooding caused loss of life. The twentieth century priority has been to completely prevent tidal flooding. The Woolwich Barrier and the raised river defences along the Thames has made this dream ninety-nine per cent effective. Industrialisation in the nineteenth century engulfed most of the river but the Sea Reach and Lower Hope still retain a little of the feeling of estuary wilderness.

From below Gravesend to Teddington Lock there is about 54 miles of the tidal Thames. This powerful grey estuary runs through the great city of London, and also right through the heart of English history. The Tower of London was built beside the Pool of London to guard the centre of the kingdom from attact from the sea. Further up river Westminister became a royal centre of power and, with the building of the Houses of Parliament, the birth of democracy. It was one of the German princes brought in to be king of England who lead to the modern pronunciation of the Thames. He could not say the original Anglo-Saxon river name of 'thames', so that the court, not wishing to give offence, switched to the modern pronunciation. The River Thames in Connecticut is still called by the original pronunciation while English children in rural areas in the 1920s were still taught the old name of the river. This change may be the reason why the men who worked on the river always called it the London River and would not have any thing to do with the modern name.

My first memory of the Thames was in 1951 when my parents took me to see the Festival of Britain on Bankside. This Festival was an attempt to recreate the great spirit of the Great Exhibition of 1851. For me the Festival of Britain was of little interest accept for the fact that we went for a trip out on the Thames and saw the famous racing barge *Sara* which was lying on a buoy in the river. I thought the Thames was a very unwelcoming river, trapped between concrete walls surrounded by people who had little contact with it.

The Festival of Britain was a warning that technology was about to sweep away the industrial pattern that had been created in the Victorian period. The relentless march forward for progress and change, for better or worse, was already well underway. I did not realise that the most of the London dock industry was going to completely collapse in the way it did, but I did know that sailing barges carrying cargoes under sail would only last a few more years. I wanted to experience working on a barge under sail and in 1956 went as mate on the *Xylonite*. When we went up the London River the docks in the upper reaches were still going at full blast. Although the water was foul, the traffic on the river made it alive and exciting.

A decade later it was still dirty and covered with drifting wood when we sailed with Tony Winter on his barge *Lord Roberts* up to Tower Bridge. It was 'tide time' when the locks into the docks opened and there was plenty of activity around the Royal group of docks, but above Gallions Reach we sailed past miles of empty silent wharves. It was as if someone had switched a light off. In a decade the great port had died.

The next change I remember was when I boarded the barge *Redoubtable* at Woolwich Arsenal in 1972. She had been one of Mitchell's ammunition barges, but had been sold to become a yacht. Our skipper Hedley Farrington had seen the river in its grimy prime before 1939 when he was skipper of the sailing barge *Gertrude May*. We spent the night on a buoy out in the tideway and Hedley was really fascinated that the river was clean enough for wild duck to land and feed.

We were witnessing the London River recovering from a century of appalling pollution. Until the 1870s the London fishermen who supplied the capital had worked from Blackwall, Greenwich and Woolwich. Then sewerage pouring straight into the river drove the fishermen down to Gravesend and Leigh. The Victorians corrected this by building sewage treatment plants and the river below London was still reasonably free of pollution until about 1930. Then new and far larger factories and chemical works poured their effluent into the tideway. At the time there was a massive world recession and factories meant jobs for people so no one in authority dared to suggest stopping them. By the time I went on the Thames in 1957 it had been at its height as a totally dead waterway. If anyone fell in and swallowed the water it was so toxic they would have been lucky to survive.

Although the river has become cleaner, it has sadly lost much of its traditional working vitality. When Len 'Jack' Faram 'came afloat' on the London River as a lighterman in 1951 there were 3807 registered freeman on the river. The massive lighterage industry ran on Victorian lines into the 1960s. All this started to change rapidly when coal dropped out of use as a source of power. Bulk cargoes had always been the backbone of the trade into the docks, but the first major freight to go was coal and then bulk cargoes were replaced by containers. The docks, the life blood on the old East End of London, closed as the trade drained away and the whole river's industry fell like a pack of cards. In 1996 I spoke to Jack at the Transport on Water Association office near the Albert Dock and there were then only about 180 men working as lightermen on the river. On the London river the term lighter is not used, all towed flat bottomed craft are barges and if they have sails they are sailormen.

When I started to write this series of books I was keen to record the sailing barge era, but have since realised that I have been recording the demise of waterborne commercial traffic along the whole of the east coast. The decline of the dockland port of London is the most dramatic. In 1914 the docks and wharves of London gave employment to around 100,000 men, but sixty years later almost all of these jobs had gone. There are many reasons why the old London dock and wharf system died, leaving mile after mile of empty derelict dockland. The upper river port might have stood a better chance of continuing if the dockers had not been quite so keen on striking, but for the large container ships of the later twentieth century, London was in the wrong place to be a port. Most of the trade to the Thames moved down to Tilbury while Southampton and Felixstowe, which are closer to the container ship routes through European waters became the main container ports.

Tilbury and many of the riverside wharves are still successful operations, but where commerce has died out it often leaves a lifeless water front. The Thames was, until the mid-Victorian period, the major yachting centre in Britain and it is still a most interesting river to sail on. Above the bridges rowing has brought life back to the tideway, but below Tower Bridge the river is seen as a backdrop to the new housing developments. Many of the old waterman's steps have survived but there is little encouragement for people to use the river. True Greenwich tried in the 1970s to start a festival linked to river activities. While in about 1993 the Erith Riverside Festival was started to get local people interested in the river. These, and the Great River Race, and many more are good events, but the Thames should be the major sailing centre of the east coast, not the river everyone wants to sail away from.

Many of the facts about the old London River have been recorded by the Society for Sailing Barge Research. In about 1967 I used to go to their meetings at the 'Pilot Inn'. Recently I returned to this hostelry to find it had been updated for a more affluent society, but I remember it as of Victorian pub with tiny rooms and customers who coughed a lot. Outside the massive East Greenwich gas works lit up the sky for miles around and beyond this was the great waterway of the London River.

It was Hugh Perks, who had been a mate in the barges, who introduced me to this society and in recent decades he has done a great deal of research into east coast shipping. Tony Farnham, also of the S for SBR, has kindly allowed me to draw on his vast collection of postcards. He grew up at Greenhithe and played around Everard's barge yard. At fourteen he joined their sailing barge *Greenhithe*. Over the following four years he was mate on the sailing barges *Cambria*, *Sara* and *Lady Mary*. The first two were coasting barges, but the *Lady Mary* traded in the river with such freights as spare tractor parts for export from Dagenham up to ships in the docks.

Another mine of information about the river is Paddy O'Driscoll who went in 1959 as mate in the barges trading from the London docks to the east coast ports. She stayed until 1970 when she left the *Northdown*. Since then she has been editor of local magazines including 'Bygone Kent' and I am very grateful to her for reading through this book .

The great recorder of sailing ships, Rick Hogben has collected many post cards of the London River and kindly allowed me to use them. I have to thank Dave Standen for talking about creeks above Hole Haven. John and Helen Skellorn were a fund of knowledge, not just on the Gravesend Sailing Club, which John joined in 1938, but on the whole lower river.

On Mucking Creek I have to thank Bernard Hipsey who grew up near the creek where he still lives, also the Thurrock Local History Society. Others who have been most helpful are Bonita

Chamberlain of the Erith and Belvedere Local History Society, Bob Aspinall of the Museum in the Dockland Project. George Skidmore on Barking Creek and on the Greenwich area Rodney Hucklesby and Peter Kent. Because they thoroughly understood the river I have found the books of A.P.Herbert and L.M.Bates very informative. The Port of London Authority have willingly helped with many enquiries. On commercial shipping I thank Alan Bennett and the author and photographer Jack Gaston, who is the expert on tugs.

On the 'rowing river' above the London bridges I have to thank Dick Hodges of the Thames Anglers Preservation Society. This Society was formed in 1838 to prevent commercial fishermen from over fishing the upper tidal reaches. Also Jeff Merrall of the Francis Francis Club who was extremely helpful about the upper river which he knows so well. On the hire trade and traditional boats Mark Edwards is the authority. He moved down to Richmond Bridge Boathouse in 1991 to take over hiring and then continued boat building there.

David and Elizabeth Wood read through the upper river section and it has greatly benefited from their considerable local knowledge. Their home now is near the Twickenham Embankment but they have spent a life time observing the river. Elizabeth grew up at Barnes in the days when it was still safe for children to wander along the banks of the Thames while David knew the docks and worked near Blackfriars. Between them they have done a great deal of work for the Inland Waterways Association and the Thames Barge Sailing Club.

For general background information I would like thank Marnie Brown, Simon Read and Doug Deas. For illustrations David Green for his beautiful drawing of Richmond lock, Ken Lockwood for his excellent barge drawings and my daughter Caroline Southernwood for giving up time from the demands of a family and career to help with this project. Geoff Cordy is to be thanked for the photographic work. My wife Pearl has shared with me the excitement of exploring this river. The one thing I found had not changed was the unmistakable aroma of the tideway foreshore.

RS
Ramsholt

Source of illustrations

Tony Farnham 1, 3, 7, 8, 20, 22, 24, 26, 27, 34, 35, 38, 43, 45, 46, 51, 59, 61, 67, 73, 103, 115, 130, 136, 137, 142, 152. Rick Hogben 2, 21, 23, 25, 37, 42, 53, 64, 89, 95, 101, 102, 110, 111, 122, 123, 132, 144. M. J. Gaston, 4 ,92, 94, 96, 97. Gravesend Sailing Club 12, 13, 14, 15, 16. Basil Emmerson 10. National Maritime Museum 11. David and Elizabeth Wood 17, 116, 118, 119, 120, 127, 128, 129, 131, 133, 134, 135, 138, 140, 141, 145, 146. Hugh Perks 18, 19, 69, 81, 82, 83, 114, 117, 121. Bonita Chamberlain 28, 29, 30, 31. E. V. Scott 36, Graham Hussey 41, 106, 107. A. Mahoney 44, 47, Paddy O'Driscoll 48, 58. PLA 9, 49, 52, 62, 71, 78, 104, 105, 150. K. C. Lockwood 54. Courtesy of Museum of Dockland Project 60, 63, 72, 75, 90, 109. Eric de Mare 65, 74. Jack Faram 66. Wapping Group 76. E. H. Cole 77. Doug Deas 79. Ron van den Bos 91.Great London Record Office 126. Francis Francis Angling Club 147, 148, 149. Mark Edwards 151. Remaining photographs either taken by the author or from his collection.

David Green's drawing of Richmond Lock 1996.

Chapter One

BELOW LONDON

1. The Chapman lighthouse off Canvey Island at the lower end of Sea Reach. The Lighthouse first showed a light in 1851, but from Roman times there had been concern about the Chapman Sand which was a danger to vessels entering the Thames. The last lighthouse keeper, F. H. Roberts left in 1956 and as the tide was scouring under the lighthouse's seven legs it was pulled down and replaced by a buoy.

2. The 'Lobster Smack' Inn beside Hole Haven in about 1912. The 'Lobster Smack' got its name from the smacks which delivered lobsters to be stored here before being taken up river to Billingsgate fish market. The wall around Canvey was built by the Dutch after which many of them stayed to farm the land. In 1648 there were over two hundred 'low Countries Strangers' living here.

3. Sailing barges in Mucking Creek, Stanford le Hope about 1910. The Thames sailing barges with flat bottoms and spritsail rig were very cost effective because they could get into the shallow creeks and required only a crew of two. A local 'huffler' often helped to row and poke the barges up creeks. In the early nineteenth century, sailing barges went into Mucking Creek for the farm trade and by 1870 Ambrose Ellis' sailing barges were working out of this creek with grain. The gravel merchant J. L. Wall also had three sailing barges transporting gravel to London from his pit. Gravel was taken on a horse drawn railway from the pit down to the wharf. After Ellis' fleet had been sold in about 1932 the buildings on Stanford Wharf were pulled down.

4. Cory's tug *Swiftstone* towing barges with containers with rubbish into Mucking. Larger tugs would have brought the barges down from London and then, as it is very shallow, the *Swiftstone* took them over the mud flats at high water. This is a fairly typical river lighterage tug, she was 91 gross tonne, had a 670hp engine and was built in 1953.

2

5. The sailing barge *Portlight* squaring away into the Sea Reach during the 1996 Passage Race between Gravesend and Harwich.

There had been a rather sad era in the 1950s as the number of barges trading under sail dwindled away. The following decade was more hopeful as people bought barges and restored then back to sail. A few were used as yachts and holiday charter barges, but increasingly it was the big companies using barges for promotion work which kept them in the best order. For several decades there were around thirty barges sailing, but by the 1990s many wooden barges which had not been rebuilt had to be abandoned and the number of barges in existence began to fall. In 1996 there were twenty-three barges sailing.

6. Andy Harman's sailing barge *Edme* in the Lower Hope just after starting the Gravesend-Harwich Passage Race in 1996. This race was first sailed in 1978 when the *Mirosa* covered the sixty five miles in around seven hours forty minutes, but in 1996 the *Edme* broke this record by making Harwich in six and half hours.

Barge racing on the Thames, officially called matches, were started in 1863 and played an important part in the sailing barge development from rough river craft into very good sea going vessels. The last race for working barges on the Thames was sailed in 1963, although in the 1970s barges raced up to Greenwich, and the Thames Barge Race from below Gravesend was revived in 1995.

7. The champion class barge *Veronica* off Tilbury Power Station. The series of barge races between 1953-63 were a publicity battle between two great Thames estuary shipping owners, the Everard family and Maurice Gill's London and Rochester Trading Company. In the 1955 race Everard's *Sara* was beaten by Gill's *Sirdar* so they decided to create an even faster barge. Everards did up the *Veronica* with a massive sail area just to take part in the Thames and Medway races. The *Veronica*, a wooden barge built by Shrubsall at East Greenwich in 1906 had been lying at Greenhithe for several years with water flowing in and out of her hulk. A Champion class was started for Everard's *Sara, Veronica,* and *Dreadnought* and Gill's *Sirdar*. The Champion class was the ultimate development of the flat bottomed spritsail barge. It was short lived because when the Everard brothers died their champion barges were scrapped.

8. Tilbury Dock about 1920 showing the original entrance to the left with Tilbury Hotel, built in 1886 and destroyed by bombing in World War II, beside it. The East and West India Dock Companies joined forces to build Tilbury Docks in 1886, but for several generations it was seen as a white elephant. When ships grew too large for the London Docks the main Port of London moved down to Tilbury. Northfleet Hope riverside container terminal at Tilbury received its first vessel *Encounter Bay* in 1978 and facilities were constantly being updated. In 1990 47.2 millions tonnes passed through the Port of London.

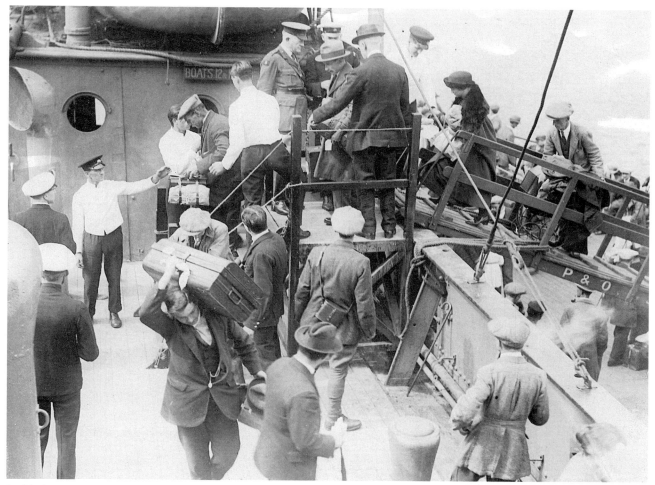

9. Emigrants boarding the P & O branch line 13,033 ton steamer *Ballarat* at Tilbury in about 1925. The Port of London was then the centre of the British Empire, a global trading net work which had taken about three hundreds years to build up.

10. The tug *Sun II* towing the replica *Godspeed* past Gravesend in 1985 after her ceremonial departure from Greenwich. This replica had been shipped over from the United States and was sailed back to Virginia. She was re-enacting the voyage of 1606 when Captain Smith sailed from Blackwall Pier to North America with *Susan Constant*, *Discovery* and *Godspeed* to make the first English speaking colony in North America. Many voyages of exploration and settlement started from the Thames.

13. The crane at the Gravesend Sailing Club around 1906 with some of the founder members Herbert Winder and Billy Edwards. It was said that with this crane they were never certain whether the boat would come up or the crane go down. The Gravesend Sailing Club, when it started in 1894, would have nothing to do with the grand yachting scene and did not have a commodore, but had a Captain and Mate as its chief officers. Originally the club members met in various public houses in the town, but they seem to have fallen out with the landlords so they moved to their present Club House near the Canal Basin lock in 1904.

Opposite Top. 11. The full rigged ship *Clarence,* a Blackwall frigate owned by London shipowner Richard Green, anchored off Gravesend in about 1860. The swim-head stumpie barge alongside would have been putting fresh victuals aboard ready for a long ocean voyage. Ships were towed down from the London docks to take on final provisions, and the last passengers, before being towed to The Downs where they made sail for their voyage. Many emigrants bound for the New World had their last contact with their homeland from the anchorage off Gravesend.

Opposite Bottom. 12. The club house of the Gravesend Sailing Club in about 1904. This club house is still being used although most of the furniture has changed.

Yachting was introduced to Britain on the Thames by King Charles II in 1660 after the Dutch gave him the yacht *Mary*. In the eighteenth century the Cumberland Fleet started their races at Blackfriars, but as the dock system expanded yachting moved down river. In 1810 yacht racing starting at Gravesend and soon the grand yacht clubs became established on the water front. Gravesend, linked to London by steamers, grew up as a fashionable spa and resort. By the 1880s the volume of commercial shipping on the river began to make yachting difficult. The centre of yachting moved to Cowes but until World War II the grand yachting season still started in the Thames with racing from the Lower Hope round the Mouse and back to Gravesend. The royal cutter *Britannia* won her first race here when she was brand new in 1893.

14. Members of the Gravesend SC in a yacht's cabin in about 1905. The large gaff cutters and yawls were owned by the professional and trades people of Gravesend and they invited other members of the club to go along and crew for the weekend and for cruises. As it was impossible to sail against the strong Thames tides weekend cruises had to be carefully planned. On a high tide early on a Saturday the yachts came out of the Basin and went down to the Medway while if it was a midday tide they could only get to Hole Haven.

At the end of the season it was a custom of the club to meet down at the 'Lobster Smack' for a supper. Often members took punts and guns and went off wildfowling. This grew into the club's Duck Supper which was originally held at the 'Kynoch Hotel' on Canvey.

Opposite Top. 15. Richie's *Vivid* being sculled over the stern into the lock at Gravesend Basin about 1907. The *Vivid* was probably built in about 1860 as one of the smaller Gravesend bawley boats and was then sold to become a yacht. After several rebuilds this little bawley was still sailing in 1996.

Opposite Bottom. 16. The former Goldsmith 'iron pot', a steel hulled barge, *Scotia* being towed out of Gravesend Basin in 1953 on her last voyage before being converted to a lighter at Maldon. Iain Mackenzie had bought the *Scotia* out of trade and rigged her out again for sailing. While she was being rigged out in the Basin several members of Gravesend SC built small yachts in her hold, in fact on her first outing there was still an unfinished hull down in the hold.

17. Clinker built shrimpers at Gravesend about 1900. Later boats fitted with boilers to cook the shrimp were called 'boiler boats' which was corrupted into bawley.

18. Bawley boats *Thistle* and *Providence* at Lower Bawley Bay, Gravesend in about 1947 The bawley boats which fished from Gravesend were used to catch shrimps as far up as Erith in the 1920s, but then pollution drove them down river to work in the Sea Reach. The last bawley at Gravesend was Bill Sutherland's *Thistle* which was sold when he died in 1970.

19. Ship handling tug *Cervia* at the Gravesend landing stage about 1952. The 105ft 233gross ton 107hp *Cervia ex-Empire Raymand* was owned by William Watkins Ltd.

20. The paddle steamer *Mermaid* off Rosherville. Early steamers brought passengers down from London to the Rosherville Pleasure Gardens, but by World War I there was a network of routes carrying summer holiday makers to resorts all round the Thames Estuary. The *Mermaid* was one of the last steamers owned by the Thames Steamboat Co which ran between Westminster Pier and Rosherville and in the summer down to Herne Bay.

11

21. Northfleet Creek about 1910. The Creek ran from the lower end of Northfleet Hope up to the fresh water Fleet which came from Spring Head. The sailing barge *Dunstable* was laid up here in 1946 and the creek was later filled in. Northfleet Creek is one of several London River creeks which have been closed to navigation. This was a great mistake because it meant there were fewer places on the tideway for people to keep boats. The people living in the Thames valley must be protected from flooding caused by high tides, but the flood defences have made a very bland river.

22. The training ship *Worcester ex Exmouth* being towed past Northfleet in 1978 on her way to be broken up in Holland. Built in 1904 she had been moored at Greenhithe as a merchant navy training ship. She was the last of a long line of ships moored in the Thames as prison hulks and training ships.

The Beach, Grays

23. Grays in 1907 with women and children using it as a resort. The great sadness is that many Thames side towns have turned their back on the river.

In this view there are nineteen sailing barges including one stackie. Grays was the home of the Goldsmith family who in 1905 owned 147 Thames sailing barges, the largest fleet. Goldsmith's fleet were 'seeking' barges in the coastal and river trades, but they lost the cement trade in 1932. After the World War II post war boom finished Goldsmith's suddenly ceased trading in about 1949 and the fleet was sold very quickly.

Goldsmith's yard is on the right, but the barges are lying at the corn merchants Cole and Lecquires' Pier Wharf. They sold their last barge, the wooden *Henry* which loaded 100 tons, at the same time as Goldsmiths so that Grays, which for a century had been alive with sailing barges, suddenly had an empty foreshore.

24. Wouldham cement works was operational from 1876-1976. The creek in the foreground was dammed off above Wouldham works, but there had been a steam mill here until about 1860.

Barges, Dartford Creek.

25. Sailing barges in Dartford Creek. In 1907 there had been about 2090 sailing barges working in the Thames and the coasting trade. By 1930 this number had about halved. As they lost their traditional trades many barges were sold off cheaply to become yachts or houseboats. The number of working barges was down to six hundred by 1939 and had halved again by the time World War II had ended. Most of them finished by 1960 and only *Cambria* carried freights under sail until 1970.

26. Barges above the lock in Dartford Creek about 1910. During the nineteenth century, industry grew up around the London River creeks so that they could utilised water transport. When the London docks system started to be wound down in the 1960s the whole water transport infrastructure collapsed. Dartford and Crayford Creeks still had motor barges such as *Decima* and *Xylonite* coming in the 1960s. Until about 1985 small oil barges and 100ton steel barges being towed to Crayford.

27. The Causeway at Erith about 1900.

28. Erith High Street about 1910. Sadly this pleasant waterfront was pulled down in 1960.

At the beginning of the nineteenth century Erith was a Thames side fishing village, but both industry and leisure moved down river. The Corinthian Yacht Club moved down to Erith in 1872 and its members had large yachts with paid crews which raced to the Nore and back. However industry and pollution caused over crowding on the river and this club moved to the Medway. Erith Yacht Club was started in 1900 and local people have been racing and cruising from here ever since.

29. Erith about 1925 with the flour mill dominating the centre of the waterfront. Industry had taken over the whole water front in the late Victorian era, but in 1937 the Erith Urban District Council bought the flour mill and pulled it down in order to create the Riverside gardens with access to the river.

At the bottom right can be seen barges lying off the former Stone's barge yard at 100 High Street. John Stone was manager of the Erith brick works and became so interested in improving the stowing space on sailing barges that he started the barge yard here. At that time sailing barges were tiller steered. In 1873 soon after Robert Stone had the barge *Anglo-Saxon* built she was fitted with a steering wheel. Stone claimed this was the first barge to have a steering wheel.

30. Messrs Parish's Ballast Wharf at West Street, Erith about 1930. Erith at this time was then handling more dead weight tonnage than any other town between London and Southampton. The largest of the lighterage and shipping firms operating from Erith was Wm Cory and Son. This company was formed in 1896 when several large coal importing firms merged into one unit. They operated 5000 railway trucks, 1500 barges, 28 tugs and 35 steam ships supplying coal to the country south of the Thames. Cory's lighters were popular with the crews of sailing barges because they were able to moor alongside at night and help themselves to coal for their cabin stoves.

31. Sailing barges at Ballast Wharf, West Street, Erith in about 1900. The Ballast Wharf appears to have been built in 1808 when sailing ships came down river from London and took on ballast, extra weight to give them stability when they sailed with a cargo. The Ballast Wharf was still there in 1965, but like the huge Cannon and Gaze's flour mill in the distance, this has all gone.

32. The Cunard liner *Mauretania* passing Erith in 1939. At the time the 36,655 ton *Mauretania* was the largest ship to visit the Port of London and this was a trial run to see if she could operate from King George V Dock, but World War II started soon afterwards and she never returned.

33. The 27,155 ton Shaw, Savill and Albion motorship *Dominion Monarch* bound down river past Greenhithe for New Zealand in 1939. On the left are two Nautical Training College ships. The wooden training ship *Worcester II* was here from 1876-1946 and the clipper *Cutty Sark* was moored here from 1938-51.

34. The sailormen *Sara* and *Cambria* on Everard's yard, Greenhithe being fitted out for the 1955 Thames Barge Match. Here F.T.Everard and Sons Ltd had built and owned sailing barges and then progressed on to building up the largest fleet of British motor coasters. Including river craft the Everards had about three hundred craft at about the time this photograph was taken. Racing sailing barges became a hobby for the brothers Will and Fred.

35. The sailing barges *M.A.C.* in Rainham Creek about 1911. This sailorman was owned by Henry Covington of Battersea. At this time there were 1700 riverside wharves between Gravesend and Brentford. Most of them relied on barges and small coasters.

36. The barge *Gwynhelen* discharging ballast at Dagenham in 1930 for the building of the new Ford car factory which was built on the open marshland. The jetty was built by John Mowlem and the barges were unloaded using the grab in just a few hours. This was then the cutting edge of technology because before this the barge crews had to discharge by hand.

37. Looking across Barking Creek to the Town Quay about 1908. Early in the nineteenth century this creek was one of the major fishing centres in Britain with smacks sailing from here to the North Sea fishery. On the left is the Barking Corn Mill and about 1750 a tide gate was fixed here keeping the water back so that barges could get up to Ilford. In 1851 Barking had 220 smacks, the world's largest fishing fleet, but the last well smack returned from the Faroe Islands in 1880.

38. A sailing barge passing through the Barking Bascule Bridge which was pulled down in 1929. The first spritsail barge built at Barking Creek was in 1810 and the last one in 1899.

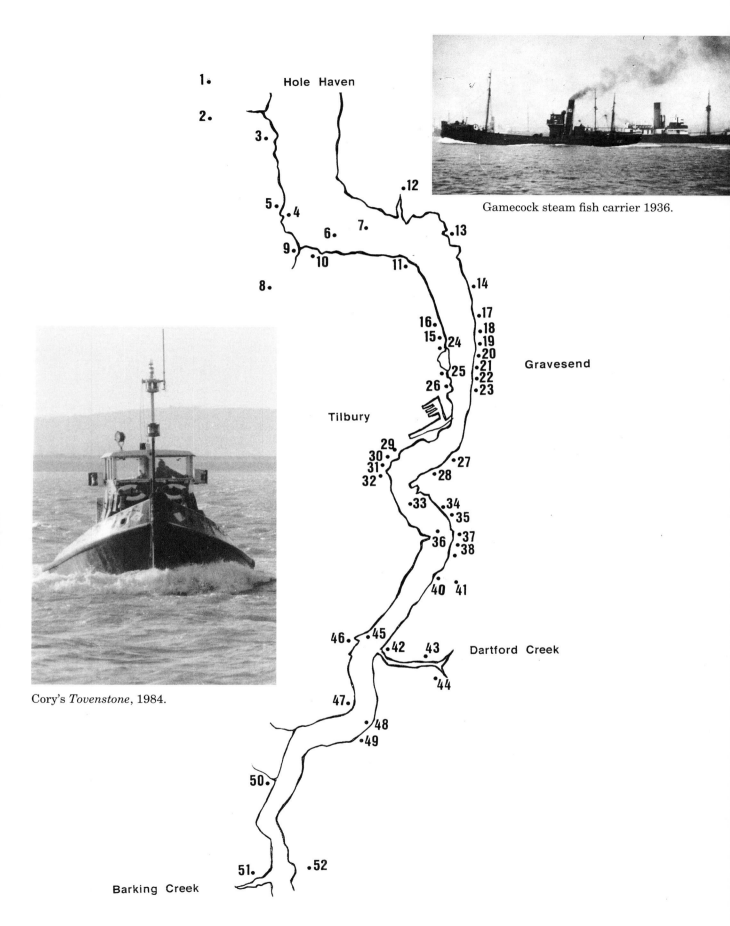

Gamecock steam fish carrier 1936.

Cory's *Tovenstone*, 1984.

Hole Haven

1.
2.
3.
5. 4.
6. 7. .12
9. .13
.10 11. .14
8. .17
16. .18
15. 24 .19
.20
25 .21
26. .22
.23

Gravesend

Tilbury

29
30 .27
31 .28
32
.33 .34
.35
36 .37
.38
40 .41

46. 45
42 43 Dartford Creek
.44

47.

.48

.49

50.

51. .52

Barking Creek

SEA REACH TO BARKING CREEK

1. The Wat Tyler Country Park, opened with its marina in 1984. The building here had been an MOD laundry for World War I. The crane at the marina was for unloading powder barges. This area was an island in the marshes until the Dutch, who had already reclaimed Canvey after 1637, also reclaimed these marshes. The Pitsea Hall Fleet was dug to create soil to build the river walls. There were at least six wharves above Hole Haven. Sailing barges went up to Vange and Pitsea in the 1930s. The last wharf was used by Cleanaway until 1987. They were stopped from bringing London rubbish up here because the paper blew out of the open hatch barges.

2. Fobbing Wharf. Used by sailing barges and dammed off after the 1953 Flood.

3. There was barge traffic up Shellhaven Creek until it was dammed. First American oil landed near Shellhaven in 1880. This whole riverside area was developed as oil storage.

4. Earl's Hope. One of the few pieces of natural saltings left for wild life in the Thames. The name Hope appears to be a very old word meaning river crossing place.

5. Curry Marsh jetty is in the oil refinery. In the 1890s the Safety Explosives Co manufactured blasting explosives here and shipped them out over the jetty.

6. The PLA would not allow power vessels carrying explosives in the Thames so by 1890 there were powder hulks moored in the Lower Hope and sailing barges then took the explosives or ammunition up to ships in the docks. T.F.Woods of Denton Wharf, Gravesend operated a fleet of 'powder barges' which had a red band painted round the hull. When the PLA rule was abandoned in 1957 ICI sold the powder barges and hulks.

7. Until 1951 sailing barges, lighters and motor barges loaded on the ebb tide with ballast from a dredger working in the Lower Hope and Sea Reach. It was claimed that dredgers had caused subsidence which created cracks in East Tilbury parish church.

8. Mucking, site of a Migration Age Anglo-Saxon settlement. In the early Bronze Age a hill top fort was built here and there seems to have been a settlement until the early Anglo-Saxon period. The settlement was probably here because this was the first sheltered place the Thames could be crossed. The early Saxons appear to have had a military camp here. Possibly to watch out for raiding ships coming into the river.

9. Mucking Creek. Mucking named after the Saxon chief Mucca. In around 1905 90ton stumpie barges drawing 5ft were going up to Mucking Church. The head of the creek was closed off when the New Sluice was built. Stanford Wharf at the bottom of Wharf Road had coal in and corn out. In 1890s Ambrose Ellis was operating a fleet of sailing barges from here and had his own barge repair yard and granary, hay store and crane. About 1932 Ellis' fleet sold, wharf buildings and cottage pulled down. Only the orchard survives. In 1905 J.S.Wall opened the Warren pit and sand was brought down on a horse drawn railway line to the wharf just inside the creek mouth. In 1919 Samuel West's sailing barges took over the ballast work to the London wharves. West's pits and barges were sold to Surridge's S.T.S.& S and ballast was shipped from the creek until about 1948. In 1932 Surridge's East Essex Reclamation Scheme built a jetty above the creek and London rubbish was brought in. Surridge's dumped World War II concrete barges in the creek in about 1955 which caused the channel to move.

11. Coalhouse Point Fort. There was a blockhouse here in 1588. Battery in 1799 to guard the port of London and the stone fort was built around 1870.

12. Cliffe Creek. In the 1920s sailing barges came in here to load mud for the Northfleet cement works. Parish wharf at the head of the creek where in the 1960s Chad Dowling started a boatyard.

13. Cliffe Fort built by Henry VIII and rebuilt by General Gordon of Khartoum.

14. Shornmead Fort. The Elizabethan blockhouse was just down river. In the 1860s Shornmead and Coalhouse were turned into stone forts which could have created murderous crossfire for any ship trying to enter the Thames.

15. Site of Tilbury Collier Station 1923-77. About 1840 the Lord Mayor of London who was by Royal Charter the Conservator of the River started to control the sailing colliers coming into the river. Bad weather held up the colliers and when the weather improved hundreds would arrive on the same tide and their skippers would jostle for a berth in the Pool of London. When steamers took over the coal the factors still wanted to know which ships had arrived in the river. In 1950 the station reported 8000 colliers to the coal exchange.

16. Tilbury Power Station. The last coal burning power station on the Thames. Between here and Battersea there were seven coal burning power stations.

17. 'Ship and Lobster'. The original start to the Thames sailing barge races in 1863 was at Erith, then a yachting centre, but in 1894 the start was moved down to the 'Ship and Lobster'.

18. Gravesend Basin. In 1824 a canal with a two mile tunnel in it was built linking the Thames to the Medway. However it was not a success as barges could sail round faster than they could go through the canal. Wells built his last yacht, *Westerly*, at their yard just down river of the lockgate in 1937. Yard destroyed by a delay mine in World War II. Gravesend Rowing Club 1878.

19. Port of London Authority Navigation Service. Formerly just up river of the Royal Terrace Pier was the wharf and barge building yard of Samuel West. Reformatory ship *Cornwall*, a 74gun, teak man-of-war built at Bombay in 1815 as *Wellesley* sunk off Gravesend in World War II.

20. The site of a 1540 blockhouse is in front of the 'Clarendon Hotel' and other blockhouse site was at the lower end of the Promenade. The Elizabethan defences included a boom across the river between Gravesend and Tilbury Fort and batteries on river bends. During World War I there was a pontoon bridge across the river a little higher up river.

21. Anchor Cove or Bawley Bay. Formerly the base of the 'boiler boats' which went shrimping between Erith and the Sea Reach. St Andrews Waterside Mission Church opened in 1871. The Mission went out to emigrant ships and when they sailed the bells were rung. The last sound many people ever heard of the motherland.

22. Up river of the Town Pier The Short Ferry to Tilbury is still operating, but the Long Ferry went out when the railways came in. The Long Ferry sailed at low water and hoped to make Billingsgate on the flood tide. However if there was a head wind the trip took much longer than six hours. The open sailing Long Ferry was a tilt-boat as the passengers slept in straw sheltered by a tilt on hoops. 'Amsterdam' pub, mentioned in the sea shanty, was at the bottom of the High Street until 1954. There were stairs here for the watermen who took passengers out to the Long Ferry. Gravesend watermen rioted when the pier was built.

23. Until 1939 the Bath Beach in front of Clifton Marine was popular for swimming. Last Gravesend skiff builder was William Warner. Watermen would hitch a tow down to the estuary in order to get aboard and ship first and get the work of mooring her.

24. Bill Melloy Creek, Tilbury, closed off about 1980 when the flood defences were heightened because of the Woolwich Barrier. Referred to as 'Bullmorois' and in 1823 as 'Bilmery' Creek.

25. Tilbury Fort. The blockhouse at West Tilbury was started by King Henry VIII in 1540. Both Henry VIII and Elizabethan I came down river in the royal barge to Tilbury to review their troops. This was the first place that London and the royal dockyards could be defended.

26. Tilbury Ocean Stage. Tilbury-Gravesend car ferry closed when Dartford tunnel opened 1963, second tunnel 1980.

27. Site of Northfleet Dockyard. William Pitcher moved down from Blackwall to start the dockyard and launched his first ship the Indiaman *Royal Charlotte* in 1789. By 1825 when he went out of business, Pitcher had built 27 naval ships and 26 merchantmen for the West and East India trade. Pitcher's sons William and Henry reopened the yard in 1839 and it became the largest shipyard on the Thames and the largest dry dock in Britain. The yard closed in 1860 and part of it became a cycle factory. In about 1924 Bowaters bought the site and built a paperwork's on it. During World War II concrete Manusell Towers were built here and then towed out into the Thames Estuary to become anti-aircraft forts.

28. Tunnel surviving from Roshervilla Gardens, last of the English pleasure gardens, 1837-1900 and briefly opened again in the 1930s. Thomas Bevan started making cement here about 1865 and began building sailing barges beside it. In 1997 the Blue Circle cement works was the last of six lower Thames cement works in operation.

29. Thurrock Yacht Club was started in 1946 and is on the site of an old coal wharf. Just up river is the abandoned jetty of corn merchants Cole & Lecquire.

30. Grays Creek which in the eighteenth century went further inland.

31. Goldsmiths Wharf. Bruce Timber Wharf 1900-1980. T.W.Ward shipbreakers 1920-1976. Grays steel jetty demolished. Grays Chalk Quarries jetty demolished. Maltings demolished about 1960.

32. Brooks cement works 1890-1919. Area around 'White Hart' built up with housing 1990-1996, such as Bruces Wharf, Genoa Quay and The Spinnaker.

33. Fiddler's Reach got this name because the sailing ships nearly always came up against a south westerly head wind here and had to tack backwards and forwards.

34. Black Duck. A barge wharf which has completely gone. John Bazley White started a cement works at Swancombe about 1855 and started a sailing barge building yard at the Black Duck. In 1882 the *Black Duck* was the first barge built here and many of J.B.White's other barges were named after birds.

35. Empire Paper Mills Wharf used to discharge pulp for the mill. Until about 1950 Stevedores, dressed in cheese cutter hats, 'choker' neck scarves and with hooks in belts, used to wait at the top of Greenhithe causeway to be hired by the day for unloading the pulp bales.

36. The training ship *HMS Worcester* was moored off Greenhithe. This was run by the Thames Nautical Training College which was started by Richard Green of the Blackwall yard in 1861.

37. Greenhithe riverside started at the down river end with W.Crouch, waterman's yard, 1996 Thames Side Services. Then the Causeway which used to be known as the Pier and had its own Pier Master. Then Tester's Greenhithe Lighterage, which included Neptune Cottages which housed their workers. Then Everard's yard, now the Mariner's Haven house estate.

38. There used to be a wooden causeway behind the 'White Hart'. When Sir John Franklin sailed in 1845 with *HMS Erebus* and *HMS Terror* to try and find the North West Passage he spent his last night in England ashore at the 'White Hart'. Franklin and his 129 officers and men were never seen alive again.

39. Globe Wharf. This wharf and the upper end of Greenhithe High Street all demolished.

40. The Johnson and Kent cement works were up river of Greenhithe.

41. Stone Church, 'the Lantern of Kent' because the sailing ships used it as a landmark when coming up river.

42. Eighteenth century Long Reach Tavern was destroyed by fire in 1957. The Tavern once stood alone in the marshland and it was a favourite place to stage prize fights. The fans of bare knuckle fighting came down from London by wherry. Once there was a ferry to Purfleet from here.

43. Dartford Creek. Open saltings until the Enclosure Act of 1601 when Dartford and Crayford Creeks were walled off. To improve barge traffic to Dartford the main creek channel was straightened in 1844. About 1896 a lock was built to help barge traffic, but by 1986 this was left open because there was no trade into the creek. Flood barrier at the creek mouth necessary because the closing of the Woolwich Barrier creates abnormally high tides in the lower Thames.

44. Crayford Creek. There was an Elizabethan iron works making armour at the head of the tidal creek and in Victorian times the Vitbe Flour Mill. Rutters, who owned the brickwork's had 20 wooden sailing barges built here starting in 1877 and ending with the *Juniper* in 1902. In 1926 there were three wharves in the creek.

45. A Neolithic settlement site on the foreshore from when the sea level was about 4ms lower than modern times. Animal bones found include horse and ox, the extinct fierce wild cattle.

46. Mar Dyke. After a gunpowder magazine was established here in about 1760 the lower Mar Dyke was dug out to let barges in. Later the stream was canalised so that barges bringing muck from London and taking corn back could get up to Rosette Fen and each farm had a dyke leading up to it.

47. Coldharbour. 1996 largest trade on the Thames was Cleanaway moving London refuse to their Rainham site. They had two tugs and 41 purpose built barges. Nine barges sold after Westminster Council ended contract for moving refuse from Governor Dock, Chelsea. 1500 tons a week brought from Battersea and 2000 tons a week from Bow Creek, two miles up the River Lea.

48. The eastern end of the bight of Erith Ranks was known as the Anchorage. Around 1800 up to fifteen East Indiamen were seen anchored here waiting for a fair wind. With all the shallows and difficulties in the channel they could only sail for an hour at the top of each tide. It sometimes took three days to work a ship from here up to Blackwall or Deptford holes from where barges took the cargoes to the London warehouses. To improve dredging in the channel, the power over the river was given to the Thames Conservancy in 1857.

49. The southern end of Erith river between Whitely Terrace and the river was the site of Erith Gardens. There was also a hotel and pier and the town was a small riverside resort. In the late nineteenth century the railway wharves and lines were built here and the whole area became a massive depot for coal brought in by sea from northern England.

50. Rainham Marshes. For a mile along the foreshore are remains of oak and yew from a prehistoric forest from the time the Thames valley was settled about 10000BC.

51. Dagenham Breach. In 1707 a high tide threw a 400 ft wide gap in the river wall. Many attempts were made to close the Dagenham Breach because the tide washed soil through which choked the channel up to London. Repairing the river wall became a national issue. The whitebait feast started here when the Commissioners made a stately river procession to the Breach House to inspect the repair work. Later the whitebait feast moved to Greenwich. When the breach was finally closed it left behind a mile long lake which in the nineteenth century was known as the Dagenham Subscription Lake and city anglers had country cottages here .

52. In 1997 tidal barrier was being built in Barking Creek just above Hand Trough Creek. Just above the barrier on the east shore is Battery Wharf which in the nineteenth century belonged to the fishing smack owners Hewett's. They also had their shipyards and wharves further up the creek in the little dock, filled about 1996, below the Business Village. In 1996 37 people, of which 6 were full time fishermen, were licensed to eel fish between Tower Bridge and Leigh. The PLA will not allow eel fishing above Tower Bridge and most of the eel fishing is done below Barking Creek.

53. The marshes here were reclaimed by making 'innings'(river wall). A great tide in 1527 flooded the Plumstead Marshes and it took eighty years to reclaim all the marshes again from tidal waters. New town Thamesmead for 60,000 people started in 1963.

The ford Canvey Island.

Chapter Two

DOCKLAND TIDEWAY

39. The 1475 grit dredge and sand carrier *Bowbelle* entering Galleons Reach in 1989. This was thirteen days after she had collided with the 46grt Thames disco passenger boat *Marchioness* near Blackfriars Bridge. The *Marchioness* sank at once with the tragic loss of 51 lives. The *Marchioness'* sister ship, *Hurlingham* , was steaming along side and passengers smashed windows and managed to save 28 people in the water. The *Bowbelle* was sold abroad in 1992 and broke in two and sank near Madeira with the loss of one life in 1996.

In the background is the remains of Becton Gas Works, once the world's largest coal burning gas works. Becton at one time used 5200 tons of coal a day, all brought by sea from the north of England.

40. A bottle nosed whale ashore at Woolwich in 1899. It is believed that whales going south from the North Sea can miss the Straits of Dover. They turn east too soon and swim up east coast rivers looking for a way through.

In the background on the left is a tiller steered sailing barge, while to her right is a 'swimmie ', a sailing barge with sloping bow. A type built mostly in the first half of the nineteenth century, as a cheap form of hull construction.

41. The sailormen *May* and *Spinaway C* leaving the King George V lock in 1958. The barges, loaded with grain, were going out into Gallion's Reach to start their passage back to Ipswich. It took under twenty four hours or several weeks, depending on the weather.

42. 'Tide time' (high water) at the main entrance to the Royal Docks in 1965 with the tug *Sun I* towing a ship out stern first so that she would point down Gallions Reach. At high tide, the dock locks were opened and the river was alive with shipping. The company owned, ship handling tugs towed ships in the tideway, while the smaller PLA tugs just worked in the docks.

The Port of London Authority was formed in 1909 when some 600 independently owned wharves and four large, highly competitive dock companies, which operated above Gallions Reach were all placed under one authority.

43. *HMS Thunderer* being towed down river after she was launched at the Thames Ironworks, Bow Creek in 1911. The slipway in Bow Creek was angled so that when a ship was launched she went out into the river. This was the last large ship built on the Thames. The *Thunderer* was towed down to the specially constructed Thunderer Jetty in Long Reach for completion. Small coasters were being built until 1939 and dumb barges until about 1980.

44. Barges lying on the buoys at Woolwich about 1956. These were known as 'Starvation buoys' because the crews were paid by the freight and drew no money while waiting for a cargo. The skippers were sculled ashore by their mates and they telephoned the owners for orders. A small shop nearby sometimes took messages saying where the next cargo was to be loaded. After World War II the owners would phone Mrs Riley and she would go down to the foreshore and shout the name of the barge so that the skipper knew he had to phone the owners to see where he was going to load.

45. The Woolwich Free Ferry seen from North Woolwich with the ferry *John Benn* crossing in about 1925.

48. Dick Norton and his watchman and general helper Fred Bayly at his barge yard in East Greenwich in 1961. Dick Norton's father and uncle had built the sailing barges *Scout and Scud* and in 1916 they built the *Serb* here. Dick ran the yard until he died in 1973.

Opposite Top. 46. Aboard the Woolwich Ferry in 1922. Just down river is the jetty used by the Sun tugs and behind can be seen the masts of sailing barges lying on the Woolwich buoys.

Opposite Bottom. 47. Skipper Bob Wells bringing the Silvertown Lighterage sailorman *May* alongside Silvertown in 1968. The wooden *May* was built in 1891 and carried grain from the Royal Docks to Ipswich under sail until 1963 after which she became a promotion barge.

    In the background on the left are the barge roads. The PLA put down buoys, screwed into the river bed, which were leased to companies to moor their barges. The PLA had a buoy at the mouth of each creek and dock so that barges waiting for the tide to go in could moor there and the lightermen could get 'a step ashore' and return on the next tide. Before the PLA laid the buoys, the lighterage barges were anchored.

49. The Union Castle Company's *Llandovery Castle* (II) entering the West India Dock. This 14 knot twin screw 10,609 ton liner was built in 1925 for the East African service and was scrapped in 1953.

West India Dock was opened in 1802 and was the centre of trade to the Caribbean in sugar, rum and hard woods. The West India Dock closed in 1980 after which the sugar trade was concentrated at Tate and Lyle's Silvertown on the Woolwich Reach.

50. One of the Victoria Steamboat Company's excursion steam off Blackwall in about 1900.

Above. 51. A steamer passing the Royal Naval College at Greenwich about 1907. The barge anchored in the foreground is a sloping swim head 'lug-boat' which was probably a 'sandie'. These barges went down river and anchored under the lee of a point, Coalhouse Point off Gravesend was a favourite place, and dredged silver sand with a leather scoop which was lowered down for the sand to wash into it. The sand was sold in London to go on tavern floors, a very old practice, and for foundry castings.

The flat bottomed craft used on the Thames from the earliest times had no connection with the Dutch barges. By the eighteenth century London River barges had developed for rowing and were used to discharge ships moored in tiers in the Pool of London. The westcountry barges with simple square sails took freights up into the fresh water Thames. By the mid-Victorian period the flat bottomed spritsail barges had progressed on from simple swim headed river barges into fine sea going craft. Because these sailormen had leeboards to allow them to sail against the wind they were called 'grippies' on the London River, but were 'spritties' on the coast.

52. A Welsh and a Dutch crew rowing ashore after the 1996 Great River Race with Greenwich Naval College in the background.

53. The 'Ship Tavern' at Greenwich in 1910. This pub held whitebait feasts and was destroyed by bombing in 1941. In 1954 the site was dug out as a dock for the clipper *Cutty Sark* .

Opposite. 54. K. C. Lockwood's drawings of a typical steel London River barge being 'driven'(rowed) on the tide. As the tide in the London River runs at about four knots the lighterman had to row the barge's faster than this in order to control them. The key to the London River barges success was the budget under the stern which acted as a fixed rudder. When under oar the lighterman pulled on the oar to push water against the rudder to steer the barge. The lightermen called their craft barges, although they were often called lighters or dumb barges.

A 50 ton 'punt' barge was rowed by one freeman. The next size up needed a freeman and boy apprentice while the 180 ton barge required two freemen. The last company to drive barges commercially on the river was E.W.Taylor of Dunbar Wharf until about 1963.

From the medieval period until the 1960s the whole port of London depended on the use of barges, but there was not a system for mooring them within the docks so that lightermen just made them fast anywhere. The situation was often chaotic, particularly in the Surrey Commercial Docks, and it was almost impossible to find open water to move a barge. Only those who have served an apprenticeship and become Freeman of the Company of Watermen and Lightermen could take a commercial craft on the London River between Tilbury and Isleworth. This Company grew from the guild started in 1514 by King Henry VIII to make the water born traffic on the Thames safer. The Watermen were always a powerful lobby on the river and managed for many years to prevent more bridges being built in order to give the wherrymen ferrying work. When the first West India Dock Act was written in 1799 the Watermen managed to force in the 'free water clause', allowing them, as they had always done on the tideway, to load over the side of any ship without paying the dock owners. The free water clause had to be taken on by all the subsequent dock companies and this meant that barges, so long as they did not load at a wharf, could load anywhere free of charge. Shippers moved as much freight as possible over the ship's sides into barges rather than go through the company's more expensive warehouse system. This meant that goods could be handled very cost effectively in the Port of London, but it helped to kill the dock system because of the colossal loss of revenue.

Steel London River Barge

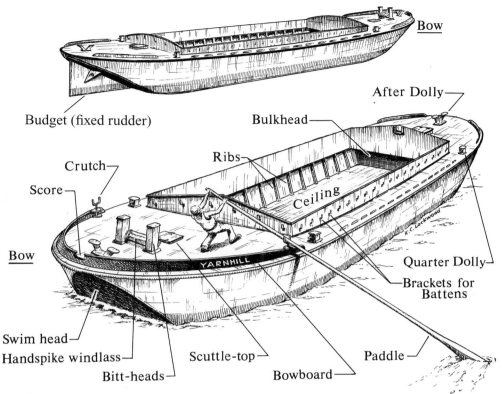

Budget (fixed rudder)

Bow

After Dolly

Bulkhead

Ribs

Crutch

Score

Ceiling

Bow

YARNHILL

Quarter Dolly

Brackets for Battens

Swim head

Handspike windlass

Scuttle-top

Bitt-heads

Bowboard

Paddle

K.C.Lockwood

Hatch Covers (when used). Either—Full span curved
Or—Half span with ridge beam.

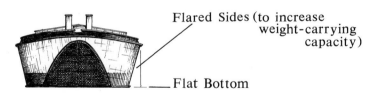

Flared Sides (to increase
weight-carrying
capacity)

Flat Bottom

Bow View

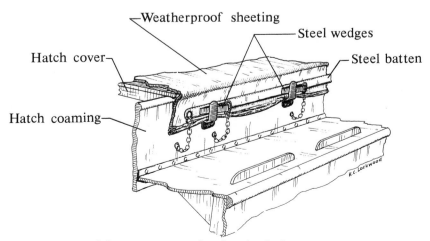

Weatherproof sheeting

Steel wedges

Hatch cover

Steel batten

Hatch coaming

K.C.Lockwood

Method of securing hatch cloths

55. Blackwall Reach 4.30am June 1973 and Reggie Coombes is driving a barge back down river. Reggie is keeping close to Blackwall Point because in order to keep control lightermen never allowed their barges to go into the bight of a bend. He had 'pulled up' (rowed) this 50 ton 'punt' to the Greenwich Festival to demonstrate the art of moving a barge on the tide. A year later a group of lightermen formed the Transport on Water Committee and started the annual Barge Driving Race.

56. The motor barge *Roina* in the Blackwall Reach with Canary Wharf in the background, 1997. Although the nineteenth century dock system had gone the Port of London at this time was the ninth largest in Europe, handled 50 million tonnes a year and gave employment to around 37000 people.

Above. 57. Royal Navy aircraft carrier *Ark Royal* lying at Greenwich in 1988.

58. Ken Everest, umpire of the barge driving match, aboard the tug *Merano* in 1978. The regalia he is wearing shows he has been a winner of the Doggett's Coat and Badge Race. This race for watermen was started by the popular actor Tom Doggett in 1715. Doggett seems to have had a soft spot for the watermen who rowed him across to the theatres on the South Bank. This is the oldest rowing race in the world.

59. In the Inner Millwall Dock goods are being loaded over the side of a ship into 180 ton barges. The dockers handled the cargo, stowing every bag by hand, while the lightermen were responsible for seeing that the barges were 'trimmed' and sheeted up ready for the PLA tugs to tow away. At 'knocking off time' the lightermen just moored up to the nearest craft, often preventing others from moving.

Opposite Top. 60. The barge *Helford* being 'driven' by a waterman and apprentice in the Limehouse Reach off Cyclops Wharf, Isle of Dogs in 1949. The old lighterman used the expression 'under oars' while 'driving' a barge meant rowing into a head wind by tacking across the tide stream like a vessel under sail. However since the 1950s the term 'driving' has meant rowing a barge.

In the medieval period imported goods could only be landed at the 'legal quay' of Queenhithe, so that the king could extract a levy. The term lingered on so that in the nineteenth century 'quay lightermen' were the ones who worked the import and export cargoes, usually with barges with hatches and a tiny cabin aft. The quay lightermen were hired by the day although in practice they usually worked for the same company. The 'rough goods' lightermen who handled the open barges which dealt mainly with coal and rubbish were hired by the week.

If the lightermen were rowing a barge on the tideway at night they just had an oil lamp up in the bow. An over night shift was a 'thgin' ('night' backwards) and if they went for a twenty-four hours shift it was a 'bag job' because they took a bag of food. After the Dock Labour Scheme was started, lightermen had regular wages.

61. Looking across Limehouse Reach to Millwall with waterman's skiffs in the foreground. The sailormen in the background are lying on buoys waiting for freights. Behind the anchored sailorman is Morton's Sufferance Wharf on Millwall. Morton's were the largest employers in Millwall and their barges collected food stuff from the docks. This view was taken in about 1935 but Morton's barges went on to be some of the last driven on the tide.

Opposite Top. 62. A tramp steamer discharging sugar into lighters in the London Docks about 1950. These are Tate & Lyle barges which had numbers not names. One of these barges is now the Thames Sailing Barge Club's *Sailorman*. Here the whole cargo is in bags which had to be loaded by hand on to slings in the ship's hold and reloaded by hand in the barges. It was a slow and dirty task and physically demanding for the dockers who worked in the docks and the stevedores who discharged the ships which were moored in tiers in the tideway.

In about 1914 100,000 men worked as casual labourers unloading ships in the Port of London. The work around the docks attracted people from all over Europe to move into the East End of London. There was always a surplus of labour and the dock companies exploited this and kept down wages. The first attempt to end this system came with the Great Strike of 1889 when the dockers fought for, and won a 'tanner an hour' (six old pennies).

In the old dock system the dockers were casual labourers simply hired at the dock gates every morning. When bad weather held up the sailing ships there was no work in the East End. The introduction of steamers made the work more even, but in the world depression around 1930 the shortage of work meant that hundreds of men turned up at the dock gates when there were only a few dozen needed. The police had to be there to hold back the crowd pushing forward to get work.

The position changed after World War II when the Labour Government introduced the National Dock Labour Scheme which guaranteed a docker a job for life. The dockers in the London were some of the best paid manual workers in the world, but unfortunately this did not end the labour problems. The dockers retained their passion for fighting the management and in the 1950s a series of strikes brought the port to a standstill and did serious damage to Britain's economy. The restrictive working practices drove trade and employment away from the London River.

Opposite Bottom. 63. Lightermen on their barges astern of a tug in 1939. When tugs came in, it was still the lightermen who looked after the barges. When under tow the lightermen usually went on the tug, but some firms such as Blue Circle did not allow their lightermen on the tugs. Lightermen gathered drift wood or coal to go on their tiny stoves down in the dank barge cabins so that they could make cups of tea. The tugs were allowed to tow up to six barges and they often dropped them off so that the lightermen could 'shoot' (row) them off on to individual wharves.

The whole lighterage industry was a very cut-throat affair with the operation run as cheaply as possible. Some of the small companies such as Darling Bros sent their lightermen out without any ropes. The lightermen had to beg an old cargo sling off the dockers or rob another barge of its 'headfast'. Property was never sacred in the London River and out on the tideway it was very much a survival of the fittest. The lightermen had to use their wit to get by and it was said they had 'more face than Woolworths'.

64. The Croydon Canal with barges and timber yards under snow in 1968. This canal was one of London's unsuccessful water arteries. The nine mile canal with nine locks was opened in 1803 and closed in 1836. However the Rotherhithe end, where the canal linked up with the timber yards in Surrey Commercial Docks, was used until 1970.

Above. 66. Barges used to take copper ingots up to the Delta works, Brimsdown at the Bow Locks into the River Lea in 1979. This was the group of watermen who got together to form the Transport on Water Association which tried to save the lighterage industry. They are Jim Woods, Ron Livett, Peter House, George Asbey, John McSweeney and Jack Faram.

The stumpie *Lady of the Lea,* built in 1931 by Hyam and Oliver, Rotherhithe was the very last sailing barge built to trade with cargoes. She was one of the War Department's fleet of small barges which brought ammunition down the River Lea from the factory at Waltham Abbey to Woolwich until just after World War II.

Hubbocks, who had a paint works near Free Trade Wharf, had the dumb barge *Alice* built in 1954 to take paint in drums up the River Lea to their wharf at Stepney. She loaded 115 tons and for the return trips her water ballast tanks were filled to make her low in the water to get under the bridges. Owen and Rita Emerson fitted a new bow and stern on the *Alice* and began sailing her as a spritsail barge in 1997.

Opposite. 65. The sailorman *M.Piper* lying in the Limekiln Dock, Limehouse about 1938. Most of the sailormen owned in London were either in the building supply or rubbish trades. The crew, usually two, did not have to include a Freeman of the River because their voyages started or finished outside the Lower Hope Point, the limit of jurisdiction of the Watermen's Company.

67. The stumpie barge *Clyde*, owned by Grays Chalk Company, off Dukes Shore, Limehouse about 1910. The *Clyde* is a 'stumpie' because she does not have a topmast. The stumpie is yet another of many types of London River barges and were mainly used to bring cement and bricks for the ever growing capital city. Some stumpies, known as 'Regent Canal' or 'Cut' barges, were very narrow so they could get through the canal locks and bridges. The Regent's Canal locks were 70ft long and 12.6ft wide. When coming back light, the barges sometimes had water let into the bilge so that they could get under the bridges.

The Limehouse shore in the background was totally devoted to river trade. This includes Sparkes barge yard and behind the *Clyde* was Dukes Shore and Steps with a barge dock. On the right is Taylor Walker's Barley Mow Brewery while the sailormen are lying a E.J.Hays Essex Wharf. Limekiln Dock was lower down.

68. The steam *Leeuwarden* at Carron Wharf on the north shore of the lower Pool of London about 1931. The children in the foreground are 'mud larks' searching the foreshore for anything useful left by the tide. The cranes could lift about one and a half tons. Tower Bridge in the distance is obliterated by 'smog', the killer fog caused by smoke from coal fires.

69. The General Steam Navigation's steamer *Falcon* being discharged at Carron Wharf about 1938. On the right a lighterman is moving a barge on Brewers Wharf which was the orginal entrance to the London Dock. The waterman in the skiff is wearing a bowler hat which shows that he was the Foreman in charge of the barges on that wharf. The larger firms also had a Labour Master, a freeman who was in charge of the lightermen Foremen.

70. The 49ft seventeenth century barque *Godspeed* in the Blackwall Basin in 1985. This American built replica sailed back to the United States to celebrate the 1606/7 voyage by Bartholomew Gosnold from the Thames to Jamestown, Virginia. The original *Godspeed* sailed with a crew of fourteen and twenty-eight settlers to make the first recorded English settlement in the United States.

Opposite Top. 71. Wapping waterfront about 1856. The London dock system was built to replace the crowded riverside wharves. In an attempt to speed up the handling of cargoes in the London docks the Port of London Authority was created in 1909 by bringing 600 independently owned wharves and four large dock companies under the control of a single authority.

Opposite Bottom. 72. Lightermen 'driving away' punts from the Surrey Commercial Dock entrance in 1949. This is off Clarence Wharf just up river of the Surrey Dock entrance and in the background are flat iron colliers at Rotherhithe Gas Works which closed in 1956. Clarence Wharf was used for aggregate until 1992 and then Bellway Homes intended demolishing it, but a strong campaign by local residents prevented them from pulling down the Victorian jetty.

Above. 73. Here a lighterman, under the shadow of Tower Bridge, is standing forward to swing the barges 'head'(bow) about 1929. Actually it was probably a posed photograph because the paddle is still locked up with a chain. While at his feet is the 'headfast'(mooring rope) attached to a 'pennant', a length of chain to stop chafing on the bowboard.

It called for great 'knowledge' of the 'sets' of the tide to control a barge on the tideway. Barges were often moved in the docks by tugs, but if there was a strong 'fair wind' the lightermen could catch enough wind by standing up and holding out a jacket to move the barge in a dock.

74. Nash & Miller's sailorman *Mona* on Pelican Wharf, just up-river from the 'Prospect of Whitby' about 1934. This firm operated the sailormen *Mona*, *Monica* and *Mary* in the ballast trade from the Lower Hope to Pelican Wharf but was acquired by Everards during World War II.

About this time one moonlight night the *Mona* was loading at the dredger in the Sea Reach and to everyone's horror the body of a woman came up sitting in one of the buckets. The driver immediately put the buckets into reverse and the lady was not seen again.

75. River traffic in the Lower Pool about 1938.

76. The Wapping Group of artists near Cherry Garden Pier about 1972. The artists are, from left to right, Charles Smith, W.Eric Thorp and Ashton Cannell. The Wapping Group was started in 1946 by a group of artists who met in the 'Prospect of Whitby'. Although it has an annual exhibition the main aim of the Group, which is limited to twenty five artists, is to paint together by the Thames. Originally the Group just painted the working river, but in recent years has been extended to the fresh water Thames and some of the ports in the Thames Estuary.

77. The excursion paddle steamer *Queen of the South* in the Pool of London in 1966. This was an attempt to revive the London excursion steam trade, but there was so much driftwood in the tideway that the *Queen of the South* kept breaking her paddles.

78. The Ivory House in St Katharine's Dock. The Thames was the centre of a great trading empire.

79. The head of St Saviour's Dock in 1950. This is the mouth of the River Neckinger which in medieval times belonged to Bermondsey Abbey. In 1554 there was a water mill at the head and meadows around the river. Most of the warehouses and mills were built between 1840-1900. To prevent the dock from being totally choked by moored barges there was a Dock Master who stood at the mouth and directed lightermen. There were grain warehouses on either side and builders merchants at the top.

Below. 80. Tugs towing barges through Tower Bridge in about 1910, while on the left a lighterman is driving a barge up on the tide.

LONDON. TOWER BRIDGE.

81. The Tower Bridge tug, one of Gaselee's, coming along side other tugs. Lying out side of the barge *New York* is the 65ft tug *Scottie*.

When the Tower Bridge was constructed across the Pool of London in 1894 lightermen and bargemen were worried that navigation would be hindered so a tug had to be on standby twenty four hours a day to give vessels a tow through. The only bomb which nearly hit Tower Bridge in World War II went through the space above the road and hit the Tower Bridge Tug which was just changing over crews. All twelve men aboard were killed. The Tower Bridge Tug was discontinued when Hays Wharf was closed.

82. Thames Steam Towage tug *Margaret* towing timber barges through Tower Bridge about 1938. The 70ft steam tug *Margaret* was built at Greenwich in 1896.

83. Gaselee's tug *Wasp* doing 'bridge work' towing barges through Tower Bridge. The 67ft iron steam tug *Wasp* was built at Blackwall in 1890.

84. In 1975 some fifty sail training and traditional ships arrived in the Pool of London for the PLA Clipper Regatta. This really marked the beginning of new era for recreational use on the river.

In the centre is the sailorman *Orinoco*, built at East Greenwich in 1895. She was the first to finish of the fifteen barges which raced up from Gravesend. The Portuguese barque *Sagres* and the USSR barque *Tovarish* are lying on the right. The Romanian barque *Mircea* had also been berthed on buoys in the Pool, but at low water she had swung inshore, touched the ground and gone over at an alarming angle. The crew were put ashore and her ballast tanks pumped out so that she floated safely on the next tide.

Opposite Top. 85. The Tall Ships came to the Lower Pool of London in 1989 because it was believed that with the opening of the Queen Elizabeth road bridge large sailing ships would not be able to get up river again. Square riggers on the buoys in the Pool of London are the 4 masted USSR training barque *Kruzenshtern*, the Polish full rigged ship *Dar Mlodziezy* and the Bulgarian barquentine *Kaliakra* .

Opposite Bottom. 86. The Bulgarian barquentine *Kaliakra* bound down river with her square sails set as the 1989 Tall Ships fleet left.

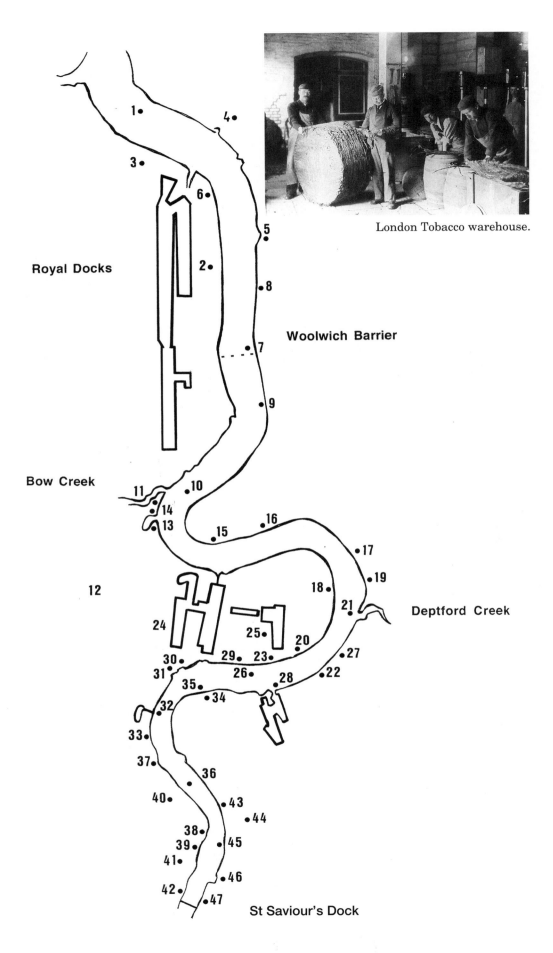

Royal Docks

Woolwich Barrier

London Tobacco warehouse.

Bow Creek

Deptford Creek

St Saviour's Dock

1 •
4 •
3 •
6 •
5 •
2 •
•8
•7
•9
•10
11 •
•14
•13
•15
•16
•17
12
•19
18 •
•21
24
25 •
•20
•27
30 •
29 •   23
31 •   26   •22
35 •   28
•32   •34
33 •
37 •
•36
40 •
•43
•44
38 •
39 •   •45
41 •
•46
42 •   •47

GALLIONS REACH TO THE LOWER POOL

1. Scene of Britain's worst peace time maritime accident. In 1878 the pleasure paddle steamer *Princess Alice* bound up river from Rosherville against the ebb was trying to dodge the tide by keeping in under the lee of the points. In doing so she crossed ahead of the collier *Bywell Castle* bound down-river and the two collided. The *Princess Alice* sank with the loss of 650 lives.

2. In the 1840s there was still a creek fed by a stream from East Ham. An area from this creek to Barking Creek was, until the nineteenth century part of the county of Kent.

3. The Royal Gallions Hotel used by passengers waiting to board ships. Originally they boarded out in the river and later on in the docks. The Royal Docks closed in 1981.

4. Woolwich Canal dug from 1812-16 to get barges up to the Woolwich Arsenal. Upper section filled 1940. Woolwich Arsenal was supplied by barges from the Royal Gunpowder Factory on the River Lea at Waltham Abbey.

5. Opposite Ferry Station was W.R.Cunis' Royal Woolwich Wharf. Their sailormen were the only ones to have black sails. H.A.Cunis of Bankside had barges with orange chrome rails, also in the ballast trade.

6. Harland and Wolff's North Woolwich shipyard employed 600 men.

7. Woolwich Barrier opened in 1982. The original marshes along the Thames acted as a flood plain, but these were all reclaimed and built over and at the same time the channel was dredged to allowed more water from North Sea tidal surges to come into the Thames. This increased flooding. There was loss of life in floods in 1928 and 1953. The Barrier prevents a tidal surge from flooding London and new high walls contain the water in the lower Thames. On the south shore is the Thames Profile Wall Mural by Simon Read which was completed in 1996.

8. Woolwich Royal Naval Dockyard established by King Henry VIII because before the nineteenth century the Ham Shelf blocked the channel above this point. Further land was reclaimed in the eighteenth century, using prisoners as labour. Dockyard closed in 1869.

9. Vaizey's Wharf. Natural gravel foreshore possible landing place for large Iron Age settlement on the hill top. 'Anchor & Hope' public house said to have got its name because barges anchored off here and hoped to find a freight. The gravel made it a good anchorage. Area developed by railway and industry. Barge building family Vaizey here until about 1947. Industry slowly pulled out of the riverside area, except for Charlton Aggregate Wharf. In 1989 houses designed by architect Joyce Lowman were built on Vaizey's Wharf. First riverside redevelopment below South Quay, Isle of Dogs.

10. There was a gibbet on Blackwall Point. Bugsby's Hole is said to be named after a pirate who was executed here. In the nineteenth century sailing colliers anchored here while waiting for a berth in the Pool. Early in the nineteenth century the smacks which sailed to Iceland for cod used to fit out on this shore. Greenwich Yacht Club founded in 1908. Blackwall Point taken up with huge Greenwich Gas Work. Redeveloped for the Millennium Project.

11. Trinity House had workshops for repairing buoys and a lighthouse for training. Sold in 1989 to the London Docklands Development Corporation. Prior's ballast barges stopped going into Bow Creek in 1996.

12. Limehouse Cut linked River Lea to the Lower Pool cut in about 1775. Regent's Canal 1820 to link Thames with Birmingham.

13. Site of the Blackwall Yard. Because of difficulties getting up to their Deptford yard the East India Company bought land at Blackwall in about 1606 and started a shipyard. In 1798 the Blackwall Yard was the largest piece of private enterprise in Europe. The famous Blackwall frigates, merchant ships trading to India were built here. The original saying 'All shipshape and Blackwall fashion' came from the smart Blackwall East Indiamen. By 1843 the yard had split into two yards Wigram & Sons with five slipways and three dry docks and R. & H Green with three slipways and one dry dock. By 1893 Wigram's had been bought by the Midland Railway Co who built Blackwell Basin and Poplar Dock and coal handling depot. The Blackwall Yard closed in 1987 and was sold to the Dockland Development Corporation.

14. The Brunswick Basin was opened in 1790 so that East Indiaman could be discharged in the safety of an enclosed dock away from river thieves who robbed ships lying on tiers in the river. The 120ft mast house was on the west side of the Basin but was pulled down in 1862. It had been a land mark for sailors returning from long voyages from the east. Brunswick Basin was filled in during World War II. Site of Brunswick Hotel which was used for whitebait feasts before they were moved to Greenwich. Emigrants waiting to go on ships to join the Australian Gold Rush stayed here. Hotel pulled down 1930. Brunswick Power Station 1952-89.

15. Just up river of the Point Draw Dock was Shrubsall's Tunnel Wharf barge yard, 1900-43. Shrubsalls were builders and owners of wooden sailing barges but it closed after bomb damage. Thomas Hughan built his last Thames dumb barge here in 1980. Jakubait's Point Wharf boatyard closed 1996.

16. Piper's Yard. James Piper and T.Scholey built and operated sailing barges in the ballast trade from here. Charter passenger boat *Calient* built at Piper's Wharf 1996.

17. Royal Naval College, Greenwich on the site of a royal palace started by King Henry VI. Royal Naval Hospital designed by Sir Christopher Wren completed in 1758 for pensioners of the Royal Navy. Closed in 1870 and the Infirmary housed seamen from the hospital ship *Dreadnought* when the ship ceased to operate. After 1873 Royal Naval College.

18. Island Gardens 1895. Potters Ferry used to cross the river here and when the subway under the river was opened in 1902 the watermen were paid compensation by the LCC for the loss of earnings.

19. *Cutty Sark*, last of the China tea clippers in graving dock, built for her in 1954. In 1884 the longitude of Greenwich (O degrees) was accepted as the prime meridian from which all time is calculated (Greenwich Mean Time).

20. North bank is where Isambard Kingdom Brunel's great steam ship *Great Eastern* was built in 1858. The slipway remains were off Westwood's wharf, two wharves downstream from the Coconut Stairs. When the area was redeveloped in 1984 more of the old slipway was discovered.

21. Deptford Creek. Prior's ballast barges from Essex cannot turn in the creek so they come up under the road bridge stern first. Pope & Bond, last traditional Thames barge yard, on riverside Wood Wharf closed 1996. Deptford Creek becomes the River Ravensbourne. Fourteen rivers flow into the Thames in central London, but only the Ravensbourne, Wandle and Lea are open and the rest are piped. London is a city of lost rivers and creeks.

22. After Sir Francis Drake's famous voyage round the world Queen Elizabeth I ordered his ship *Golden Hind* to be kept in the busy Royal Naval Dockyard at Deptford. This great dockyard started in 1485 and it closed in 1869 because wooden warships were being replaced by iron. The closure was a major blow to Deptford. The Royal Naval Victualling Yard opened in 1745 and closed in 1961.

23. The 1,100ton ship *Trade's Increase*, then the largest British merchantman, was the first ship built by the East India Company at their new yard at Deptford in 1609.

24. West India Dock, built 1802 was the first enclosed wet dock on the Isle of Dogs. Millwall Dock built 1868. After the West India Dock closed in 1980 the only quay being worked above Gallions Reach was the Victoria Deep Water Terminal, Greenwich until about 1991.

25. Millwall got its name from seven drainage windmills which stood on the river wall before the docks were dug. Open marshland until the nineteenth century docks created the new towns of Millwall, and Cubitt Town, named after Sir William Cubitt. Ten people drowned at Millwall in the 1928 Floods. Millwall community did not recover from World War II bombing. The nineteenth century docks were all enclosed by high walls. Most of the dock area was swept away in the 1980s to become the centre of the London Docklands Development.

26. Millwall barge roads.

27. When the power station was built in 1913 on the site of Roff's Wharf the remains of a great wooden ship was found in a dock. This is thought to have been the *Sovereign* built in 1509.

28. Greenland Entrance Lock. Site of Howland Great Wet Dock, dug in 1696, London's first enclosed wet dock. Later known as the Greenland Dock because it was the base for whalers. Surrey Commercial Docks were mainly used for timber imports and in 1939, 1500 deal porters and a similar number of stevedores were employed here. These docks had better labour relations than those on the northern shore. Finally closed in 1970.

29. Union Dry Dock built in 1845 by sinking the 1797 East Indiaman *Canton*. Later a slipway and barge yard.

30. Dunbar Wharf, west of Lime Kiln Dock. In the early nineteenth century this was the base of shipowner Duncan Dunbar whose sailing ships traded with Australia and the Far East. The Dunbar ships lay on tiers in the river or in the East India Dock while cargoes were discharged into barges.

31. Limekiln Creek. The lime kilns, which gave the area its name, were on the west bank. In the 1930s this was a very tough seaman's area known as Chinatown.

32. Entrance via Regent's Canal to Grand Union Canal leading to the Midlands. Branch canal to Paddington opened in 1801 and then Regent's Canal linking GUC to Limehouse Basin in 1820. The City Wharf near Sturt's lock on the Regent's Canal was operated by Henry Dodd (1801-1881), 'the golden dustman', who started the first Thames sailing barge race in 1863. Dodd had a fleet of barges which carted refuse from London to the Kent brickfields and took bricks back.

33. Formerly the barge yard of W.N. Sparks & Sons. Taken over by the lighterage firm of W.J. Woodward Fisher in 1955. This firm was later run by the redoubtable Mrs Dolly Woodward Fisher. When her lightermen argued about conditions Mrs Woodward Fisher would say 'I can remember the time when the men were made of steel and the lighters were made of wood!'. The firm closed in 1972 with the loss of 32 jobs.

34. On the south shore at Rotherhide is Nelson's Dry Dock, once the home of the Orient Line of clippers to Australia which later became part of P & O.

35. Off Odessa Street is Condemned Hole where in the eighteenth century HM Customs destroyed contraband. This continued in the twentieth century.

36. Trinity Ballast Roads. Trinity House had the right to dredge ballast from the river bed and ships came down from the Pool to take ballast aboard here. The ballast bargemen were the only men on the river who did not have to belong to the Waterman's Company. The nineteenth century ballast barges were round bowed, rather like a Humber keel, possibly even older in design than the swimhead barges.

37. King Edward VII Memorial Park was the site of Shadwell Fish Market. Free Trade Wharf originally East India Company warehouse of 1795. Later used by a group advocating free trade. Known to lightermen as the 'madhouse' because there was always chaos there. Fresh Wharf got its name because in the medieval times fresh fish were discharged here. Hubbock's Wharf just above Ratcliff Stone Stairs became a housing estate in 1996.

38. 'Prospect of Whitby' originally the 'Devil's Tavern' built 1540 and rebuilt 1777 named after a ship which traded from Whitby with stone. The quays at Wapping, Shadwell and Hay's Wharf were started after the 1666 Fire of London destroyed many of the old wharves in front of the City. In the late eighteenth century Wapping was a fashionable suburb with many fine houses, and the area around Ratcliff highway became a notorious sailortown.

39. Along the Wapping water front was Execution Dock. Around 1701 pirates, including Captain Kidd, were hung and their bodies left chained to posts for three tides. The drought of 1997 created very low tides revealing two 20ft long ships rudders on the Shadwell foreshore. These were probably from late eighteenth century 112ft long ships and were laid on the foreshore to make hard standing while working around ships.

40. London Dock 1805. Closed 1969.

41. St Katharine's Dock is a small dock designed by Thomas Telford. It was totally enclosed by high brick warehouses to prevent pilfering. Opened in 1828 closed 1968. Opened in 1974 as a yacht marina.

42. Irongate Wharf, the site in front of the Tower Hotel, was the headquarters of the General Steam Navigation Co which had eighteen cargo steamers. All the wharves along the Upper Pool had closed by 1967.

43. It is believed that the Pilgrim Father's ship *Mayflower* sailed from the reach near the 'Mayflower' public house in 1620.

44. Christopher Jones, captain of the *Mayflower*, is buried at St Mary's Church..

45. Cherry Garden Pier closed by 1981. Certain families of freemen watermen used to act as 'mud pilots'. They boarded ships at the Cherry Garden Pier to take them up river above London Bridge. Other watermen were 'dock pilots' and moved ships in the docks. The 'Angel' on Bermondsey Wall is mentioned by Samuel Pepys in his diary. This was the site of a royal manor house built by Edward III in 1350.

46. St Saviour's Dock. Site of Jacob's Island in Victorian times a notorious den of poverty and vice.

47. Anchor Brewhouse started in 1789. Anchor Brewery, built in 1895, had a foot tunnel through it so that the watermen could reach the traditional watermans stairs which went down to the river. The brewery closed in 1981.

The *Royal George* off Woolwich.

Opposite Top. 87. The Australian replica bark *Endeavour* in the Pool of London, 1997. For all his three voyages to the Pacific Captain James Cook chose Whitby colliers, not Royal Navy ships of the period. For the first voyage the Admiralty purchased the 110ft *Earl of Pembroke* in 1768, one of the many ships carrying coal from the north of England down to the Thames, and converted her to the *Endeavour* at HM Dockyard, Deptford. Cook's voyages led to the subsequent British settlement of Australia.

Opposite Right. 88. Just above Tower Bridge in about 1905. The derricks on the ship are being used to discharge into barges. The two sailormen on the left were known as 'stumpies' because they did not have topmasts. They just worked between the Thames and the Medway. On the bottom right are two 'boat boys'. For the first two years of a Freemen's apprenticeship the boys just did boat work giving the lightermen and stevedores 'a step ashore'. The watermen's skiffs had a hook in the stern so that they could tow barges out to the buoys in the barge roads.

Chapter Three
UP THROUGH

89. The two vessels on the right are palingaaks, Dutch eel boats, which brought live eels to Billingsgate. This buoy was known as the Dutch Mooring and there was a tradition that so long as a Dutch eel boat lay there they could have a free berth. It was said that the Dutch had been given this privilege because they had rendered great service during the Great Plague of 1665.

 The palingaaks used to come across from The Netherlands, lie in Hole Haven and then sailed up to the Pool when their cargo of eels were needed. In 1910 the Thames had become so badly polluted that the steamer *Thames,* on the left, was fitted with a water filtering plant so that eels could be stored on her. The Dutch eel trade finished in 1932, but the palingaaks and steamer sometimes lay here until 1938.

90. The Pool of London on the evening of September 7 1940, the beginning of the London Blitz. A thousand German aircraft bombed London and this was the start of fifty-seven consecutive nights of bombing. The Port of London was severely damaged and there was an appalling loss of life. A third of all the port's warehouses and transit sheds were destroyed, but the Port of London continued to operate. The Blitz damage was the beginning of the end of the nineteenth century port in the upper Thames although it continued to be the world's largest port into the 1960s. The port of London had a massive system of wharves, waterways and canals through which freight passed in barges. Also from the docks freight was transhipped into sailing barges for coastal ports. When the upper river docks and wharves closed this whole system slowly crumbled away.

91. The Polish ship *Jaruslaw Dabrowski* discharging at Mark Brown's Wharf just above Tower Bridge in the Pool in 1968. Hays Wharf Group took over the wharves along the south shore of the Pool of London which was known as 'London's Larder' because food stuff was imported here. In the 1870s the china tea clippers were discharged here, while in the inter war years Russian ships came.

92. The 1995 Barge Driving Race in the Pool of London with the Transport & General Workers Union barge *John Smith* in the lead. In this race barges are rowed by four freemen and two apprentices of the Waterman's Company the seven miles from Greenwich to Blackfriars Bridge.

After starting the Driving Race in 1974 lightermen began to discuss how far a barge could be rowed. In 1978 Ron Livett and his sons Stephen and Christopher started at Denton with the 50 ton punt *Fantasia* to see how far they could drive in four day time flood tides. The first day they met a fresh NW wind in the Northfleet Hope and had to 'wind' the barge to come round on to each 'fetch', in fact they turned to windward in the same way as a sailing barge. The first day they reached Erith, the next day the Fountain Buoy, Wapping and finally reached Eel Pie Island. They had covered 45 miles and been driving for 20 hours, 30 minutes. In 1979 Ken Hawkridge with five other Freemen set out to see how far they could row the 34 registered ton barge *Jane* on an ebb tide from Teddington Lock. In 6 hours 21 minutes they covered the 19.1 miles down to Tower Bridge which they just reached as the flood started.

93. Essex smacks alongside the Billingsgate Fish market in 1972. In Victorian times the Essex smacks used to sail up to Billingsgate with the first of the season's oysters and this race was revived in 1972 to publicise oysters. Billingsgate stood on the site of one of the gates in the wall of the Roman City of London. In 1982 the Fish Market moved to the Isle of Dogs.

Opposite Top. 94. The tug *Mersina* towing the barges back from the 1995 Barge Driving Race. The *Mersina* is a lighterage tug used by Cory Lighterage for towing refuse barges. One of the last of the traditional lighterage tugs was the *Friston Down* built for Humphrey and Grey Lighterage in 1964. Probably the last dumb barge built on the Thames was launched by Thomas Hughan at Greenwich in 1980. At the time there were still 1,116 towing barges on the river and sixty-three tugs.

About 1960 the lighterage companies on the London River alone handled 13 million tonnes a year. This tonnage dropped dramatically during the great London River trade decline to 6.7 million tons by 1969. By 1980 this had fallen again to 2.7 million tonnes and the hauling of London rubbish had become the major trade on the river. However there was still considerable trade and in 1990 5.4 million tons were handled by riverside wharves above the Thames Barrier. 1996 saw another decline when the vessels with cement to Hurlingham finished and the Westminster rubbish contracts ended to Grosvenor dock.

Opposite. 95. Waterman on his skiff, Bankside about 1913.

ST. PAUL'S CATHEDRAL & RIVER THAMES, LONDON.

BEAGLES'
POSTCARDS.

96. The tug *Rana* towing a dumb barge and a hopper barge in King's Reach and just about to go under Hungerford Bridge, 1997. These are Alan C. Bennett Co's craft which moved soil from the Jubilee Line near the Festival Hall. The 700hp 99 gross tonne *Rana* was built in 1951.

97. Cleanaway's 800hp 92 gross tonne tug *Jean Raby* in King's Reach off Westminster Pier. This is a very traditional river lighterage tug which has been working on the river since she was built in 1951.

98. Pedlars Acre, site of the London County Council County Hall, in 1906.

99. Houses of Parliament about 1880 before this area was embanked and Victoria Tower Gardens created.

100. The shallop *Lady Mayoress*, replica of a sixteenth century Thames passenger boat built by Mark Edwards at Hampton. Gentlemen had their own shallops for water transport until horse carriages became more popular in the eighteenth century. Cardinal Wolsey had his own highly decorated barge manned by watermen in vivid scarlet jackets. When Wolsey went down river to see King Henry VIII at his Greenwich Palace he boarded his barge at York House, but would not risk shooting through the old London Bridge. Instead he landed at Crane's Steps above the bridge and was taken further by mule decked out in crimson and velvet with bronze gilt stirrups. With attendants walking in front Wolsey went down Thames Street to Billingsgate where he boarded his barge again.

101. Paddle steamer *Crested Eagle* taking on passengers at the Old Swan Pier in 1929. She had her funnel lowered to get under London Bridge. This steamer was lost at the Dunkirk Evacuation in 1940.

Above. 102. A sailorman 'bound down river' on the ebb and about to 'shoot' under Blackfriars Bridge about 1909. The sailormen had a crew of two, skipper and mate, and the third man aboard was a huffer hired to help with the rowing. Sailormen anchored in the Mud Hole below Tower Bridge and lowered their 'gear' (masts). If a barge was bound for a wharf below Kew Bridge the crew were expected to row them up on the tide, but if they were going further up, normally a tug would be hired. Jack Huggy of Bankside is claimed to have been the last Thames huffler helping barges up through the bridges and he stopped work about 1937.

103. Everard's wooden sailorman *Sara* at the Festival of Britain in 1951. Launches ran river trips from the Festival of Britain which was the beginning of the present era of passenger boats on the Thames. On the right is the Shot Tower where boiling lead was dropped down into water to make gun shot during the nineteenth century.

104. The Thames Waterman's cutter *Penelope* with Steven Redgrave at stroke with a crew of PLA apprentices going under Blackfriars Railway Bridge on the day of the 1995 Doggett's Coat and Badge Wager.

105. The start of the Port of London Challenge Cup off the Palace of Westminster in 1996. The nearest Waterman's cutter is the PLA's *Penelope* then City Barge Company *Buccaneer*, Fishermongers' Company *Royal Dolphin* and the Waterman's Company *Tim Holt* which won the race down to London Bridge. The 34ft Waterman's Cutters are traditional style racing boats designed for the Great River Race and other events. They were designed and built by Mark Edwards at Richmond, the first one being the 'Green Cutter' *Buccaneer* in 1994.

106. The wooden Ipswich sailorman *Venture* lowering her gear to go up above the London Bridges in 1954. Astern is the Tower Bridge tug waiting to take her 'up through' the bridges. By this time barges were no longer rowed up through the bridges, but some Ipswichmen still 'drudged' through the bridges. They dropped their gear and then drifted on the tide with the anchor just touching the bottom, and they used the rudder to steer them. However since many tug skippers had either been lightermen or sailormen they were sympathetic and gave a 'snatch' up. In return for this tow they received a 'drink', often taken out of the cargo.

107. The Ipswich sailorman *Venture* loading wheat shot down a canvas shoot at the Winchester Wharf in 1954. Winchester Wharf was three wharves up from Cannon Street Bridge on the south shore.

108. St Thomas' Hospital about 1895 with a deep laden, tiller steered sailorman anchored in the Lambeth Reach.

109. The tug *Tyburn Brook* towing dumb barges past Lambeth Palace in 1953.

Above. 110. The paddle steamer *Boadicea* at Lambeth Pier in 1902. She was one of a series of steamers used by the London County Council in a river bus service. Some of these steamers were built by Rennie at Greenwich and several jetties were constructed. This river service ran at a great loss and the LCC was heavily criticised for the money lost from the rates.

111. The sailormen *Magnet* and *Shah* discharging near St Mary's Church, Battersea in 1904.

Above. 112. Nash and Miller's barge yard at Nine Elms, Lambeth in about 1900. This was before the building of the Embankment and elms trees can be seen in the background. London grew as an industrial centre because goods could be moved cheaply by barge on the Thames and the numerous linking waterways. This barge yard was part of a huge system of commercial activity that slowly evolved from the medieval period so that by the nineteenth century goods came into the London docks and were moved on to factories and warehouses along the river.

113. The sailorman *Monica* which was built in 1906 and was one of fourteen sailing barges owned by Miller's at Battersea and in the general river trade. In the foreground is one of the wooden 50 ton 'punt' barges.

Above. 114. Crescent Shipping's *Blatence* and *Cadence* unloading wheat at Garton's Mill, Battersea in 1980. The craft on the inside has already discharged and would have left at high water to allow the loaded vessel to come alongside the quay.

115. The Chelsea Yacht & Boat Company's floating workshops at Cheyne Walk, Chelsea about 1934. The sailorman is the *Eureka* and by the 1950s Cheyne Walk had acquired a small colony of wooden sailormen used as houseboats including Robin Sellwood's *James Piper*.

116. The 140ft City of London barge *Maria Wood* with Bishop's Park, Fulham in the background. This barge was built in 1818 and used until 1859 for the Lord Mayor of London to make an annual tour of the river. It took eight horses to tow this barge against the stream and four with it. The livery companies started to have their own ceremonial barges in the fifteenth century. In the mid-Victorian period the last of the City Livery Companies barges were sold to Oxford University boat clubs.

117. The sailormen *Gladstone* and *Martin Luther* lying at the Atroyal Brewery, Putney about 1890.

118. The stumpie barge *Alfred* and coal barges with the new Putney Bridge under construction in the background about 1883.

119. The sailorman *W.H.Randall* at Putney draw dock about 1882. The river was the cheapest form of bulk transport.

120. The *Lucretia* and *Maplin* discharging bricks with three other tiller steered sailormen at Putney draw dock just above Putney Bridge in about 1897. The *Maplin* loaded 90 tons(35,000 bricks) from Great Wakering, Essex.

121. The wooden tiller steered barge *Peter* at Putney in the Great Frost of 1881.

122. The sailing barge *Henry & Jabez* at Chiswick Draw Dock beside 'Red Lion' in the Mall just inside Chiswick Eyot and the power station in the background in 1903. Most of the freights taken up through the bridges by sailing barges were building materials. It was said that a barge carried enough bricks for one house. Blue Circle Cement had a wharf at Brentford. In 1954 they moved to Hurlingham and had barges towed up with cement.

123. Sailormen discharging bricks and cement into horse drawn carts at the Mall, Chiswick about 1910. The dumb barge on the left appears to be loaded with pipes. There were oiser beds on Chiswick Eyot. This was common along the Thames and these willows were cut and made into baskets which were sold to the many market gardeners who sold their vegetables at Brentford Market.

124. Oxford boat crew at the 1905 University Boat Race. The Oxford and Cambridge University Boat Race is the best known rowing race on the Thames. It started here in 1829 and in 1845 was fixed on a course of 4 1/4 miles from Putney up to the 'Ship' at Mortlake.

The first major rowing race was the Wingfield Sculls which was between Westminster and Putney in 1830. From 1849-60 it was rowed between Putney and Kew and after this it switched to the University Boat Race course. The first rowing club at Putney was the London RC in 1858 and then the Thames RC in 1861. A.P.Herbert called Putney 'the heart of English rowing'.

The major race in recent decades has been the Tideway Head of the River race which the PLA restricts to 450 eights. Putney is still the home of several rowing clubs, but major racing has moved to Henley while rowing in lines at Nottingham is very popular. The Seniors still train at Putney, but most of the racing here is just done by the Juniors.

125. The Oxford crew getting their boat ashore at Mortlake above the 'Ship' after winning the 1905 University Boat race by three lengths. This race captures the public's imagination more than any other rowing race.

126. The Oxford boat winning the hundredth Oxford-Cambridge Boat Race in 1954. This races is the best knowing rowing event on the tideway and takes place in the spring on the Saturday before Holy Week.

127. Barges at Morlake about 1880. These upper river Thames barges have sloping 'swim head bows' the same as the dumb barges. A shortage of sound wooden hulls has seen the clock turn back and swim head barges are being fitted out to sail. One dumb barge rigged out is Reg Coomb's *Whippet* at Barking Creek and another swim head dumb barge the 72ft 65ton *Fertile* was rigged out as a stumpie in 1996 by Steve Brotherhood.

128. Strand on the Green, Chiswick about 1870 with the City of London barge *Maria Wood* on her mooring just below the second Kew Bridge.

129. The lug sail barge *George & Jane* at Strand on the Green. She was owned by George Jupp, a malster at Brentford who also had premises at Strand on the Green. She was one of the upper river barges which had either a lightweight sprit or a lug rig for working from the London docks up through the bridges to the towns above London.

130. Barges at Strand on the Green about 1908.

131. The 43tons sailorman *Eight Brothers* which was built at Strand on the Green. On deck are owner Mrs Peace of 307 High Street, Brentford and her eight sons. In 1897 this barge was sold to Joseph Mears of Crabtree Wharf, Fulham.

132. Sailing barge *Swift*, which was owned by Thomas Bevan of Northfleet, discharging 80 tons of cement at Kew draw dock in 1910. This draw dock was still in regular use in 1930. The timber was handed out from the barge into horse drawn carts or 3ton lorries. Barges also discharged at Strand on the Green just down river on the left.

133. A bluff bowed barge at The Hollows, Brentford about 1860 with a bargeman with stove pipe hat.

134. The Hollows in 1963 with Brentford gas works and the barge *Glencoe*.

Below. 135. The barge *Alfred* at Brentford Town Quay and another of Jupp's barges in one of the tidal backwaters at Brentford. These small barges just carried cargoes from the docks in London up through the bridges to upper river wharves. They had a light weight spritsail or lug rig on a short mast so that they could be sailed between bridges.

136. The Ferry Hotel and ferry at Brentford about 1908. The ferry from the end of Soaphouse Creek across to Kew Gardens ran until about 1935.

137. Isleworth draw dock and church in about 1905. A punt is waiting at the bottom of the Ferry hard.

138. 'The London Apprentice' and Dutch coaster *Nautilus* at Isleworth in 1971. Taylor's timber wharf closed in 1973 and some scrap iron was taken away in small coasters after this.

139. Bricks being discharged from a stumpie barge near Richmond Bridge about 1890 when the river was low before the half tide lock was built. Nineteenth century London and its suburbs were largely built of brick. This is one of the many views of the river taken by the Victorian photographer Henry Taunt who specialised in Thames subjects.

140. Barges at St Helna Wharf, Richmond about 1895. Most of the barges working to Richmond were owned by Wheeler and Downs.

141. Barges at Richmond about 1895. The trade to the draw dock at the foot of Water Lane continued until about the World War I.

142. Richmond riverside in about 1912 with the 72ft sailing barge *Plimsoll* at Town Wharf. She was here with cement from the Swale and was one of the small canal or cut barges. The watermen are working on their boats. The boat houses on the Richmond riverside were built in about 1825 for the watermen to house their skiffs.

The summer hire trade with skiffs steadily increased at Richmond and there were many disputes between watermen. To keep the peace the riverside was divided up into six Hire Stations and watermen had set days that they could operate. Until around 1860 only licensed watermen could row on the river, but as skiffs became more popular they were hired out. The hire trade decreased when the people from the East End started to take the train to Wembley Dog Racing and the watermen said that most of their trade had 'gone to the dogs'.

143. Hire skiffs on the Middlesex shore and a barge at East Twickenham draw dock with Richmond on the opposite bank about 1900. Looking through the bridge a sailing barge can just be seen on the Town Wharf.

144. Barges at the draw dock, Twickenham in 1905. Eastwood's sailing barge *Suffolk* on the right would have been bringing bricks from Medway brick fields. In the centre of the postcard can just be seen the white tablet set in the church wall showing the level of the 1774 flood water. The warehouse to the right is Bowyer's Wharf, later Champion's Wharf, which had just been built and has since been replaced by a public garden. The last commercial traffic to Twickenham were timber barges until about 1949.

145. The Thames punts and skiffs at Charlie Shore's Children's Regatta in the gutway between Twickenham Embankment and Eel Pie Island. Eel Pie Island covers eight acres and the Twickenham Embankment was built in about 1875 when progressive people wanted to tame the natural river. A feature of the Thames skiffs are the wooden tholes to hold the oars in place. These are on the saxboard, a name thought to have come from the axeboard on Viking ships.

146. The Eel Pie Island ferry on the Ham shore about 1930. This ferry was operated by the Eel Pie Island Hotel.

147. The Francis Francis Angling Club in their eight punts at the Embankment, Twickenham in 1973. Although Francis Francis, the great Victorian fish expert and editor of the *Field,* lived in Twickenham, the club simply took his name. This is a unique angling club in that members fish from punts and keep the fish alive in the wet wells. The Club was in existence in 1907 and does not have any private water but fishes between Richmond Lock and Teddington.

The punt in the foreground is the *Mary* built about 1890 as a Thames duck shooting punt. The other punts operated by the club are from 18-21ft long and 4ft beam. The club is limited to twenty members and all of them have to help maintain the punts during the closed season.

150. PLA apprentices 'port' their oars at the naming ceremony of *Penelope* at the Ham Landing stage in 1994. This 34ft Thames Waterman's cutter was the third of the type designed and built by Mark Edwards at Richmond and the second in fibre glass.

Opposite Top. 148. Dave Stevens and Les Hills fishing between Teddington Boat Lock and the Weir in a Francis Francis Club punt. Each punt is the responsibility of a puntsman and when the club meets on a Sunday morning other members draw lots to see which punt they should go out on. Until about 1965 the punts were propelled by pushing poles, but outboards gradually took over. The punts are moored Thames-style across the stream by driving in two rypecks, long poles with iron spiked tips, secured by a chain 'sinnet'. Bread bait is used to catch the fresh water fish. All the punts return to the double steps on the Embankment at an agreed time and the member who has caught the largest specimen is the week's winner. The club has the longest weekly record of fish caught in the river.

Opposite Bottom. 149. Francis Francis club members after pike near Teddington Weir. In the drought of 1976 no water went over the weir for ten weeks. It took seven years after this for fish stocks to revive and roach still had not recovered to their former size and number by 1997.

In the Victorian era the Thames Anglers Preservation Society fought a long battle to prevent professional fishermen, who lived around the Twickenham Embankment and up to Staines, from netting fish. The Society dumped old carts and spikes in the river to stopping netting, but allowed the fishermen to continue using three hooks on a line and the custom of stirring up the river with a rake to make the fish feed. The London pollution prevented fish from coming up river until sea trout reappeared in about 1968 and by the late 1970s the occasional salmon began coming up river again.

151. Mark Edwards in the Thames wherry he built in 1981. The wherries were the water taxis of the Thames from the seventeenth to nineteenth century. They had long pointed sterns and were designed to glide over the water while the Thames skiffs had transom sterns. In the Victorian period rowing clubs used wherries for racing and one of these is in the National Maritime Museum. Mark Edwards built this wherry slightly narrower than the original ones.

152. The Footbridge below Teddington Weir about 1909.

153. End of an era, burning the hull of the sailing barge *Rowland* at Teddington lock on November 5, 1970. The *Rowland* had what must have been a typical career for a wooden sailing barge. She was built in 1895, loaded 135 tons of cargo and traded until she sank in 1952. Then she became a yacht and finally a houseboat on the upper tideway.

The upper tideway has many Dutch inland waterways barges, but very few Thames wooden sailing barges have survived. The *Leonard Piper* built at East Greenwich in 1910 and the steel *Resourceful* are houseboats at Chiswick Mall. Another of the Piper barges, the *Wilfred* built of steel at East Greenwich in 1926, was a restaurant on the Victoria Embankment in 1996.

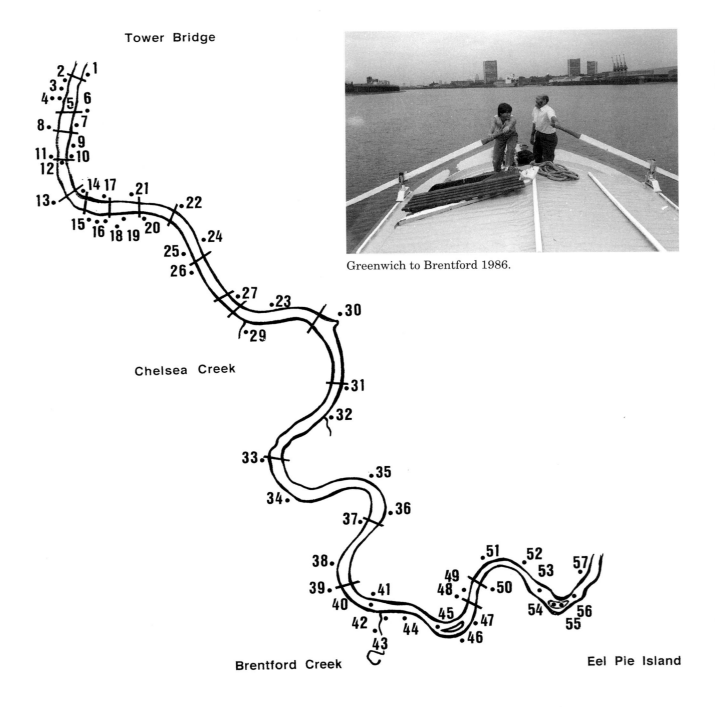

Tower Bridge

Chelsea Creek

Greenwich to Brentford 1986.

Brentford Creek

Eel Pie Island

92

TOWER BRIDGE TO TEDDINGTON WEIR

1. Tower Bridge opened 1894.

2. Tower of London. William the Conqueror started building this in 1078. Trailor's Gate where prisoners were brought in by water. King Henry VIII kept a polar bear at the Tower and it was led down to the river to catch salmon. The Tower Beach was created in 1934 with 1500 tons of sand so that the children of the East End could play there.

3. Tower Pier replaced the Old Swan Pier in 1929. Excursion steamers used to take on passengers for trips to the Thames Estuary ports until the 1960s.

4. Roman town of London from about 100AD was on the north bank of the Thames. Its river entrance gates in the town wall were at Dowgate, just below the present Cannon Street Station, and Billingsgate. The Roman quays were much further inland at Lower Thames Street. Most of the buildings between The Tower and Temple church were destroyed in the 1666 Fire of London.

5. Billingsgate. Until the 1920s steam carriers still brought fish in from the North Sea trawling fleets. In 1936 when a slight rise in the price of coal made this uneconomic, 57 steam carriers and their crews were made redundant .

6. London Bridge 1973. It is thought that there had been a Roman bridge here, then a medieval bridge slightly downstream and the third bridge, 1831-1971 was taken to Pheonix, Arizona.

7. Until about 1949 Albion Wharf, near Blackfriars railway bridge was the home wharf of Horace Cunis' sailormen.

8. Southwark Bridge 1921. Between the bridge and the 'Samuel Pepys' is Queenhithe. This was one of the medieval Legal Quays. When ships were discharged in the Pool of London all goods due for customs payment had to be landed at a legal quay. The River Walbrook, which runs up to Bucklersbury and was used by barges, is piped into the Thames below Southwark Bridge.

9. Globe Theatre opened in 1996. The original Globe and Rose Theatres of the Elizabethan period were in Bankside. The watermen did a roaring trade ferrying people across to the theatres and bawdy houses.

10. Bankside Power Station. Pre-war power station bombed during the London Blitz, 1940. New power station designed by Sir Charles Gilbert Scott opened in 1948 closed 1981. Oil fired because it was near the City. Greenmoor Wharf was Southwark Council's place for loading rubbish into sailing barges. Most of the wharves above the bridges were used to supply goods for London.

11. Cannon Street Railway Bridge, 1886. Start of King's Reach. Remains of the St Paul's Bridge closed in 1917.

12. Blackfriar's Railway Bridge, 1886. During World War II the road bridge was hit by bombs, but not the railway bridge. The remains of a flat bottom Roman barge found at Blackfriars in 1910. In the medieval period the Fleet, a small river with adjoining rivers of Turnbrookmill and Oldbourne which had wharves along them, entered the Thames near the present Blackfriars Bridge. The Fleet always had trouble with silting up which was not helped by Londoners throwing their rubbish in. In 1502 it was dredged so that boats carrying fish could get up to Oldbourne Bridge. Between 1737-65 the Fleet was arched over and runs out into the Thames near Blackfriars Bridge.

13. Rennies's Waterloo Bridge 1817-1937. By dredging the river deeper the force of the tide was increased and the early bridges had to be replaced. Waterloo Bridge 1944 designed by Sir Charles Gilbert Scott was known as the Lady's Bridge because there were so many women workers engaged in its construction.

14. National Theatre on King's Reach. South shore just down river from Waterloo Bridge was Lambeth Lead Works Shot Tower, built 1789. Dewar's Whisky Wharf. Spiller's Millenium Mill. All the waterside buildings were removed to build the Royal Festival Hall and Pier for the 1951 Festival of Britain. For centuries Londoners have thought of the Thames foreshore as being a cheap building site and kept filling in the river, making it narrower. The Coin Street Project grew out of a campaign to save Oxo foreshore. This led to a 'start from the river' water front development around the Bernie Spain Park and then on to the Stamford Wharf building.

15. The Victoria Embankment was constructed in 1869 in front of the old waterfront.

16. A set of steps which were the royal river landing place for the Palace of Whitehall are now further inland in the lawn in front of the Ministry of Defence . King Henry VIII's Palace of Whitehall was the largest in Europe and was burnt down in 1698.

17. The building of the County Hall for the London County Council started before World War I and continued 1922-1933. Closed 1986.

18. Westminster Pier and Bridge. For centuries the Waterman's Company fought off attempts to build a second London bridge, but Westminster Bridge was built in 1749. Westminster Steps had been on the north shore and Members of Parliament used these when hiring wherries. First bridge replaced 1831.

19. Houses of Parliament (completed 1860 after fire).

20. Lambeth Bridge, 1862-1929. Present bridge 1932. Lambeth Palace is the London home of the Archbishop of Canterbury, building was started in the late thirteenth century. Vauxhall Pleasure Gardens were nearby after 1660.

21. Albert Embankment 1867. Brown's Flour Mill and seven other wharves east of Vauxhall Bridge. In the 1930s Burley's and Surridge's sailing barges loaded 'rough stuff' (rubbish) from the Lambeth Council Wharf opposite the Tate Gallery.

22. Vauxhall Bridge 1926 replaced 1816 bridge. Just down steam of Vauxhall Bridge is thought to be the end of King Canute's 1016 canal. The Danish King Canute wished to be King of England and came up river with a fleet of long ships. However the city of London remained loyal to King Ethelred the Unready. Canute had the canal dug to get his ships around London, but he later managed to become King of England. In 1176 King Henry commissioned Peter de Colechurch to build a stone London Bridge and appears to have redug the canal to lower the flow of the Thames. The south entrance to this canal later became the entrance the Greenland Dock. The River Effra which runs past Brixton is piped into the river at Vauxhall.

23. In 1997 the only ship trading regularly above the bridges was *Tracey Bennett* which carried 1200tonnes between Northfleet and St Albans Sand and Gravel, Battersea .

24. Battersea Power Station built 1936. At Battersea there were two drawdocks, the Silk Factory draw dock and Church dock.

25. Chelsea Bridge 1937. Thames Archaeological Survey found a Saxon water front on the foreshore. Between Grosvenor railway bridge and Chelsea Bridge is Grosvenor Canal which was shortened when the railway was built.

26. Eighteenth century Ranelagh Pleasure Garden near Chelsea Royal Hospital. Chelsea Embankment built 1874 to prevent flooding.

27. Between Albert Bridge 1873 and Battersea Bridge 1772 and second bridge 1890 on the south shore is Ransome's Dock. The area was developed as a housing estate in 1986. Inland Waterways Association campaigned to have the lock refurbished and after the gates were opened the barge *Vigilant* berthed here.

28. Chelsea or Counter's Creek and Lots Road Power station. Chelsea Creek was the entrance to Kensington Canal which was filled in during the 1970s. Chelsea Embankment 1871.

29. Chelsea Basin owned by British Rail and used to transfer all types of cargo. Redeveloped about 1987 as Chelsea harbour yacht marina.

30. Wandsworth Bridge 1940. Wandsworth Creek and Bell Lane Creek. Bronze Age people cast offerings into Wandsworth Reach. They seem to have believed the tidal river was a masculine god which lived into modern times as Old Father Thames. Before pollution Wandsworth was a salmon fishing centre. A few sailormen came in the creek with bricks into the 1930s. In 1994 the Wandle Delta Project started to try and clear up the river. In 1997 this was the furthest point west on the Thames that rubbish was collected. Prior's ballast barges came as far as this in the 1990s. Barges drawing 10ft came up to Pioneer's wharf just below the creek and to below the bridge on the Fulham shore to Ready Mix wharf just above Swedish Wharf. In 1997 the small tanker *Bruce Stone* was still coming up to Fulham.

31. Putney Bridge. First wooden toll bridge in 1729 was second bridge on the tidal Thames. Second bridge 1887. Putney draw dock just above the bridge. University Stone is the start of the Oxford-Cambridge University Boat Race. The nineteenth century towpath started at Putney and went all the way up river to Lechlade. The two miles of river between Putney and Hammersmith are very wide and ideal for rowing.

32. Beverley Brook. Sailing barges were taking ballast in here in the 1930s. As barges had to go in stern first it was not a popular place. Dammed off just above entrance, but some of the basin remains.

33. Hammersmith Bridge 1827 and then suspension bridge 1887. Hammersmith Creek just up river from the bridge was used by barges until being filled in and the pier built there. There was considerable barge traffic to the hard in front of Queen Wharf next to the bridge. Traffic to draw dock just below the bridge and hard. Three draw docks in Fulham were Crab Tree, Swan and Broomhouse. Most of the draw docks appear to have been older than the riverside wharves.

34. Chiswick Mall draw dock. Ferry from Chiswick Steps at the bottom of Church Street across Corney Reach to Barnes. In 1997 new houses on 13.5 acres of riverside land while the Chiswick Pier Trust promoted the use of the river with a new pier.

35. Small Profits draw dock, Corney Reach, Barnes had posts for barges to moor to which seem to have been used until the 1920s. River walls built up after 1953 Floods.

36. Two draw docks in Mortlake, Bull Alley and Ship Lane mainly used by barges working to the malthouses and Mortlake Brewery.

37. Chiswick Bridge 1933. Gravel workings on the Middlesex shore became Cubitts Yacht Basin from about 1905-73. This became Chiswick Quay Marina.

38. Strand on the Green. Formerly the home of watermen and fishermen. The 'City Barge' public house was formerly the 'Navigation Arms', but the name was changed because in the nineteenth century the City of London barge *Maria Wood* was kept in a barge house on the Kew shore. Oliver's Island was the toll point when the City of London controlled the river. Later PLA office near Kew Pier. Sailing club started in l947.

39. Kew Bridge, 1758-9, 1789 and then 1903. The Hollows above Kew Bridge on the Brentford shore was the home of wooden sailing barges converted to house boats, but in 1996 these had been replaced by steel Dutch barges here and at Victoria Steps. Watermans Park opened 1983 formerly town gas works 1820-1963.

40. On Lots Ait, the smallest upper island, Thames Steam Tug & Lighterage Co Ltd, known on the river as the 'Limited', had a barge yard. Became part of Thames and General until they closed in 1980. Thames and General also known as '(Battersea) dog's home' because it was such a mixture of companies. Brentford Barge Roads just up river of Railway Dock.

41. Three ancient trackways met at the great ford at Brentford. Last freights to Brentford about 1973 were barges with paper pulp to DRG Ferry Wharf, Soaphouse Creek.

42. Marina formerly the G.W.R Brentford Railway Dock. Opened 1859 and mainly used for transhipping coal from barges to the railways. In 1918 the railway company started working barges from the river frontage as well. 1980 dock redeveloped with narrower lock as a yacht marina and housing. Amongst the considerable trade through Brentford was GWR timber for railway sleepers brought from the docks to their depot at Southall. Narrow boats brought creosote and other goods down the canal from the Midlands.

43. First locks of the Grand Union Canal to Birmingham. Low head room under Brentford High Street bridge prevented barges over 125 tons from going up the canal. E.C.Jones yard, pioneer builders of narrow boats and bantam tugs, at the entrance to the River Brent until 1992. In 1994 SPL Marine started building steel craft just above the bridge on Dock Road at the former Vokins Wharf. Originally a single lock but modernised about 1961. The ice in the severe winter of 1963 started the decline of trade to Brentford Dock and through the canal. Last regular trade was timber and Roses limejuice.

44. Middlesex shore of Syon Reach is one of the few sections of the tideway river that still has a natural bank. In 1928 a Romano-British hut site was found below the foreshore. When the City of London dredged the river in the 1770s they used the spoil to built the new tow path on the Kew shore. This was on the wrong side of the river, but they had to do this because all the old towns were on the deep water shore and the buildings obstructed a tow path. Brentford opposed the tow path because they thought it would take trade away from their town.

45. Foot ferries above and below Isleworth Ait. The Isleworth draw dock was just above the Shallows in front of the Church and is 14.87 miles above London Bridge. Inside the Ait was the Town Wharf used by sailing barges. Isleworth ferry was revived about 1994 and ran sometimes in the summer .

46. Duke's River. Traces of cill for the lockgates which allowed barges to take wheat to Kidd's Mill until about 1935. Railshead Ferry, above Isleworth Ait, closed and compensation was paid to the ferryman when the Richmond Footbridge was constructed.

47. Richmond Footbridge, sluices and half tide lock opened 1894 to control the level of water upstream to Teddington. Sluice gates are lowered and raised two hours either side of high water. The half tide lock was built to keep up the water level because so much water was being taken out by water companies.

48. Twickenham Bridge 1933. Opened on the same day as Chiswick and Hampton Court Bridges. Trace of jetty from the royal palace of Sheen (Richmond). Most of this Tudor palace was pulled down by Cromwell's Parliament in 1649.

49. In the eighteenth century Richmond riverside known as Cholmondeley Walk, after the house the Earl of Cholmondeley built about 1740, was the a fashionable place to walk by the river. Mark on a building at the bottom of Water Lane showing the height of the 1928 Flood caused by a high tide and very heavy rain. Richmond Terrace between Old Town Hall and the river is part of the Quinlan Terry development opened by Queen Elizabeth II in 1988.

50. Richmond Bridge 1777. As the river is narrow here, there was a horse ferry before the bridge which was a toll bridge until 1859. Bridge widened in 1937 and is the oldest surviving tideway bridge. Upstream of the bridge is St Margaret's Draw Dock in East Twickenham.

51. Buccleugh Gardens. In 1777 the City of London, seeking to increase their revenue from tolls, wanted to create a barge towing path along the Richmond riverside and up to Staines. In 1779 George Colman of Bath House hired men to drive away the labourers building the path. After the fighting the City Marshals and a file of soldiers were brought in, but the Duke of Buccleugh used influence at court to stop the path going through his gardens. Buccleugh Gardens bought by the council in 1938.

52. Petersham Draw dock. The first ferry plying place above Richmond Bridge was from Cambridge Park. Walter Hammerton was a local hero because he started the next ferry in 1915 after a six year legal battle with the Duke of Dysart. Hammerton's Ferry was the only one still running in 1997 after ferryman Stan Rust had just bought a new boat. Ham Ferry ran from the bottom of Orleans Road. Twickenham Ferry ran from near the 'White Swan' and was a privately owned ferry, suggesting it is the oldest, probably started by the Ist Duke of Dysart in about 1640. This was run by Sidney Cole, Harold Smoothy and then David Hastings and his sons until about 1989.

53. Twickenham Yacht Club house. This yacht club was started in 1897 after the Richmond Half Tide Lock. The lock was built because the water companies were taking so much water from the river that it effected barge traffic and summer hire trade on the upper tidal reaches.

54. Eel Pie Island got it's name because Londoners came up here to enjoy eating eel pies. The natural main channel or 'gut' ran the Twickenham side but when the river was dredged for barge traffic the straighter route was taken on the Ham shore. First public house on the island in 1736, but it had been a place of recreation before this. Bungalows and Eel Pie Island Hotel, on the main channel side in the 1920s while four boat yards on the island were mainly concerned with hiring out skiffs. Ferry to Eel Pie Island until Snapper's foot bridge was built in 1951 and a small toll used to be charged. Hotel burnt down and in 1996 the Eel Pie Marine Centre, the former Thames Launch Works, at the eastern end was badly damaged by fire.

55. Boat builder Bill Sims bought the Racing Boats yard on Eel Pie Island in 1957. At one time fourteen people were employed building wooden racing boats, but fibre glass hulls killed the demand. In 1996 George Sims and three men were fitting out fibre glass shells and only building new wooden racing boats for heavy rowers or 'coaster' boats.

56. The ferry above Eel Pie island at Cross Deep was run by Dunn until about 1945. This was a watermans' plying place where a licenced watermen operated a ferry in good weather.

57. Barges took gravel from Ham dock on the Surrey shore. After the pit closed became the Thames Young Mariner's Base. Swan Island has a houseboat colony. The former Tough's boatyard up stream at Teddington from where many 'Little Ships' set off for Dunkirk in 1940, sold to become housing. Up to 298 yards below Teddington Lock, built 1811, the Port of London Authority controls the river and above this the Environmental Agency has control. The three locks at Teddington are the limit of the tidal Thames. The Teddington Old Lock is in the middle. Beside it is the Skiff Lock which has the smallest lock chamber in Britain. On the Surrey bank is the larger 1904 Barge Lock. This is 650ft long and was built so that it was large enough for a tug towing six barges to lock in.

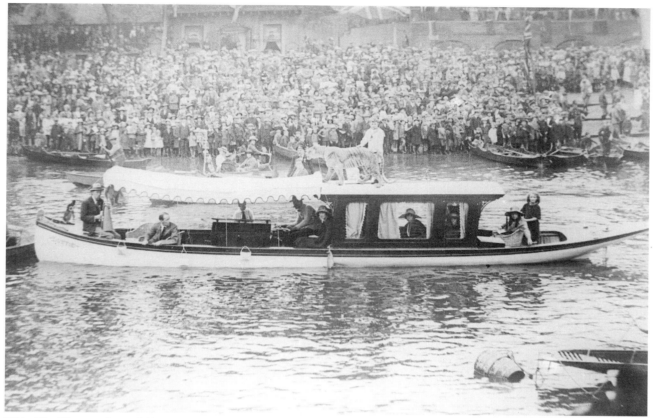

154. The Thames launch *Lottie* in about 1925.

155. Eel Pie Island Regatta.

156. The *Rose in June* in the Pool of London, 1997.

157. The Thames Waterman's cutter *Buccaneer* near Ham House, 1994.